Festivals &
Celebrations

Jim Fitzsimmons & Rhona Whiteford

Bright Ideas
FOR Early Years

Published by Scholastic Publications Ltd,
Villiers House, Clarendon Avenue,
Leamington Spa, Warwickshire
CV32 5PR

© 1994 Scholastic Publications

Written by Rhona Whiteford and Jim
Fitzsimmons
Edited by Jo Saxelby-Jennings
Sub-edited by Kate Banham
Designed by Anna Oliwa
Illustrations by Debbie Clark
Photographs by Bob Bray (page 5), Paul
Hill (page 51) and Russell Firth (page 67)
Cover design by Lynne Joesbury and
Micky Pledge
Cover photograph by Martyn Chillmaid

Every attempt has been made to trace and acknowledge the
origins of pre-published material and photographs appearing
in this book. The publishers apologise for any omissions.

Typeset by Typesetters (Birmingham) Ltd
Artwork by Steve Williams & Associates, Leicester
Printed in Great Britain by The Alden Press, Oxford

British Library Cataloguing in Publication Data
A catalogue record for this book is available from the British
Library
ISBN 0-590-53083-6

Contents

Introduction

The nations of the world each hold their own beliefs and values and these are expressed publicly through their festivals and celebrations. Some of these events are connected with religious belief and others with long-held customs and their form is often an expression of lifestyle. For children in the early years the deeper religious significance may be beyond comprehension, but the sights, sounds and everyday behaviour of children like themselves may provide comparisons they can understand. Celebratory clothes, presents, activities, tasting new foods, the colours and decorations, the music and images of other cultures can help, by comparison, to affirm the beliefs of the home.

The experiences of the early years can have a profound effect on the development of a child's attitudes and values and consequently on his or her relationship with other people. If we begin by sensitively introducing young children to lifestyles other than their own, if we widen their experience of the way people behave, we can perhaps contribute to their development of tolerance and appreciation of others' beliefs. However, a child must first be secure and confident in his or her own identity.

We suggest the attitudes expressed in this poem as a starting point for all work with children.

Children learn what they live

If a child lives with criticism,
   He learns to condemn.
If a child lives with hostility,
   He learns to fight.
If a child lives with ridicule,
   He learns to be shy.
If a child lives with shame,
   He learns to feel guilty.
If a child lives with tolerance,
   He learns to be patient.
If a child lives with encouragement,
   He learns confidence.
If a child lives with praise,
   He learns to appreciate.
If a child lives with fairness,
   He learns justice.
If a child lives with security,
   He learns to have faith.
If a child lives with approval,
   He learns to like himself.
If a child lives with acceptance
   and friendship, he learns
   to find love in the world.

How to use this book

The festivals and celebrations we have included in this book represent a number of the world's religions. They are arranged in approximately chronological order. However, many religions use lunar calendars or other methods of calculation to decide when a particular festival will occur, so their dates will vary considerably year to year, around the Western calendar. In *all* cases, please check the precise date of a festival in a current reference book such as the *Shap Calendar of Religious Festivals*, produced annually by the Shap Working Party on World Religions in Education and published by Hobsons.

The individual activities are cross-curricular and provide a variety of new experiences from familiar starting points. All the activities in this book require a greater or lesser degree of adult supervision. Many early years children may not have acquired all the skills necessary for a particular task. It may be that a child can only attempt two or three of the techniques involved, and that adult preparation or finishing off is necessary.

What is important, is that the children should practise or learn a single skill and have an end product of which they can feel proud. The youngest or most inexperienced in this age group will be able to do very little on their own, but even in short sessions of practical activity a good teacher can develop the child's powers of observation and discussion, visual perception of the work and possibly imagination too.

The individual teacher will need to determine which of the skills the children can attempt, and this will depend upon their previous experience. Obviously some of the tasks will involve greater concentration spans and several processes and these activities will be most suitable for more experienced children. However, it is possible to organise the work so that even the youngest can tackle a long task, if the job is broken up into several sessions over a week. Examine carefully the skills involved in a task, and help the children with new skills, even apparently easy ones such as the manipulation of glue spreaders, paintbrushes and scissors — correct hand positions are very important and a little assistance can help a child to achieve success. Remember that the observation and discussion of activities is just as important as the doing, and much language development can result from even the simplest of tasks.

Do try a variety of activities so that the children gain experience of many materials and techniques. With the cookery activities, for example, the children can observe and discuss the changes brought about by mixing ingredients and the effects of heating or cooling on different substances. Their senses too will be focused; on the appealing smells and tastes and the look and feel of the ingredients before and after cooking. Talk about the ongoing activity to help the children conceptualise their experiences.

Safety aspects

For most types of art and craft work, children in this age group will have an adult present to guide them and to discuss the work in progress. However, it is always wise to be vigilant where safety is concerned. Remember to store all dangerous substances and equipment well out of reach of the children. These items include some adhesives, spray-paint cans, craft knives, pointed scissors, and very small craft materials, such as lentils, peas or buttons. Even six-year-olds can inadvertently swallow such small items or push them into ears, noses or eyes. Use spray paint only in a well-ventilated area, and keep the children out of the range of the spray. Although you might let them have a go, if you guide their hands. Do be aware of the possibility of allergic reactions to certain foods by children, if you prepare any of the recipes or offer different foods for the children to try.

Encourage safety awareness in the children and any classroom helpers, for example by getting them to spot any dangerous items left unattended or asking them to carry equipment such as scissors in a safe manner. Remind the children not to put small objects in their mouths or poke friends with sharp craft materials. Even art straws can cause damage if poked in an eye or down an ear. Adhesives, paint and sand on a hard floor can cause someone to slip. Young children readily absorb safety advice in their code of rules and can be quite helpful in maintaining safety standards.

Resources

We suggest that you set up a small resource collection which will be useful for many other topics which you may look at. Parents and other members of your local community may be able to help with artefacts or advice.

You could include:

• clothes — a dressing-up box containing several types of everyday clothes worn by other cultures such as a length of fabric for a small sari, a Nordic embroidered skirt, an African robe, a Scottish kilt and so on;

• dolls — a small selection of dolls of different racial types with a selection of the same types of clothes as described above, which can be used for display or play;

• music — a collection of tape recordings or discs of music from cultures such as Indian, Oriental, European folk, Irish or Scottish dance, Reggae, African and so on;

• puppets — make a set of felt glove puppets of different skin types and a set of simple robes and accessories which can be added to make the puppets look like the kings from the Nativity of Jesus, or Moses, or Rama or St Nicholas;

• artefacts — artefacts from different cultures can sometimes be borrowed from teachers' centres or multifaith centres or you may be able to make a collection of items from the parents. Useful items might include foreign (particularly Chinese) money, divas, Rastafarian art or a menorah.

• people — try to compile a list of people in the community who are willing and able to come in to talk to the children or provide cultural information for you.

In conclusion

Let tolerance and interest be your watch words, to help prevent the ignorance and fear which cause so many of the world's problems. Above all, enjoy the activities and be prepared to learn something new with the children.

We cannot stress enough the value of praise in the learning process. All children need this vital boost to develop confidence and to become creative in their own right.

January – April

Chapter one

Many festivals and celebrations take place in the early part of the year, during the months of January to April. In the Northern hemisphere, these months coincide with the ending of winter and the coming of spring. As a result, many of the festivals celebrate new beginnings and new life after the dark days of winter and were originally intended to wake up the earth and encourage fertility in the soil in order to ensure a good crop for the coming year. Some of these festivals are simply a recognition of the fact that after the hardships of winter, the blossoming of the trees, baby animals being born, the growth of new crops and the coming warmer days, encourage an appreciation of life and a feeling of happiness and well-being.

New Year in the Western World

New Year in the Western World is celebrated in January. It is the custom to reflect on the past year and plan for the future one and people often set themselves goals called 'New Year's resolutions'.

The coming of New Year is usually celebrated by parties on 31 December through to midnight, when 1 January is welcomed by cheers and the singing of 'Auld lang syne' as the assembly join crossed hands to represent unity and togetherness.

In Scotland, where the New Year celebration is called 'Hogmanay', this is a time for family gatherings, for cleaning out the home and for making treats for the celebration. There are scones, Hogmanay oat cakes and black buns. Many people have adopted the Scottish custom of 'first footing', when a dark-haired male 'stranger', carrying a piece of coal for good luck, is arranged to be the first visitor to enter the house after midnight and by so doing brings good luck into the house for the coming year. Particular customs vary locally. In Lancashire, for example, the traditional celebration food is hotpot and black peas.

Traditional images of New Year are linked to the agricultural seasons: Old Father Time, with his scythe having reaped the events of the past year, and a newborn cherub holding an hour glass, to represent the seeds of the new one. Greetings cards with similar images are sometimes sent.

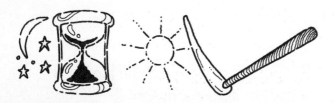

Passing years

What you need
Paper, black felt-tipped pen, access to a photocopier.

What to do
Prepare a master sheet as shown, including some small decoration round the edge for the children to add to and colour. Then make a copy of this page for each child in the group.

This is a time-consuming activity best carried out with a small group, to give the maximum opportunity for discussion. Some children at this age may know the date of their birthday, but possibly not their year of birth. This activity provides an opportunity to think about passing years and the notation involved.

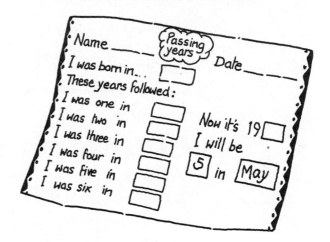

Janus models

What you need
Self-hardening clay (such as Newclay), newspaper, old tray, small scrap items for making marks, small pieces of card each with a child's name on the edge, Newclay hardener (optional), gold spray paint (optional).

What to do

Janus was the Ancient Roman god with two faces, one looking forward to the future and one looking back to the past.

Take a lump of clay, a little larger than an egg, for each child and, if the clay is wet, throw it on to a newspaper-covered surface and knead it as for bread dough until it is less tacky. Next, shape each piece of clay into a ball and squeeze a short, fat neck at the base. Stand the model heads on name cards and let the children work the features. Using any small objects, they should draw a face on each side of the head; perhaps pressing in the end of a ballpoint-pen casing to make eye shapes or the edge of a small bottle top for a curved mouth, or perhaps using an old fork to score hair marks over the head. Discuss with the children how they might make one face look old and one look young.

Transfer the heads on cards to a tray which can be kept at moderate room temperature to dry. This usually takes about three days. Treat the models with Newclay hardener for a longer lasting finish and spray with gold paint to make them look like statues. Remember always to use spray paint in a well-ventilated area.

New Year's resolutions

What you need

Tape recorder, blank tape, very long piece of paper, felt-tipped pens.

What to do

Have a discussion about the children's achievements, their daily lives and behaviour. Help them to form some ideas of what they could do to make their lives or behaviour better in any way. Help the children identify achievable small goals and, acting as scribe if necessary, write a resolution for each child on a separate piece of paper and display them.

You could tape parts of these discussions and play them back after a period of time to recall ideas and review the situation. Remember that at this early age even a fortnight is a long time.

Auld lang syne

What you need

No special requirements.

What to do

Arrange the children in a large circle and show them how to cross their hands and join them with their neighbours'. Next practise the slow up and down movement of hands, usually done in time to the song 'Auld lang syne'. Older children will be able to learn the song, 'Auld lang syne' (which is a poem by Robert Burns put to music and means, 'For old times' sake') and the youngest will enjoy the participation.

Twelfth Night or Epiphany

Twelfth Night (6 January) is, traditionally, the day when all Christmas decorations are taken down, because this is the end of the Christmas season. It is also the day in the Christian calendar which is called Epiphany, when the church remembers how Jesus was presented for the first time to people who were not Jews. The people were the three travellers from the East known as the Three Kings or Magi or Wise Men, who brought gifts of gold, frankincense and myrrh. Today, the Three Wise Men are often shown in Christmas pictures, and there may be figures of them in the Christmas crib scenes that can be seen in churches.

In Italy, this is the day on which children receive their presents, not from Father Christmas but from La Befana, a witch-like character who is supposed to fly around with presents looking for the Christ-child and, just to be sure she gives him a gift, she leaves each child she visits a present.

In Russia, there is a similar character called Baboushka, who is said to have looked after the Three Wise Men on their journey to Bethlehem and wanted to visit the baby Jesus too. However, she stayed behind to clean her house after the Wise Men left and, ever since, she is meant to have been searching for the Christ-child and leaves a present in each of the houses she visits.

The story of La Befana

What you need
A version of the story of La Befana or Baboushka.

What to do
Read the story of La Befana, or Baboushka, and let the children act it out, using cardboard crowns and the Three Kings' robes from the Christmas Nativity play or, alternatively, cloaks made from lengths of curtain material.

Taking down the decorations

What you need
No special requirements.

What to do
Leave the Christmas decorations up in the classroom until Twelfth Night or, if this is not possible, leave the role-play centre decorated. Let the children help in taking down the decorations and emphasise the need for care and safety. Collect all the decorations together and look at them. Encourage the children to sort them into sets according to different properties, such as colour, size and shape. Look at the containers in which the decorations are stored, and discuss the best way to pack the decorations so that they will be kept safe and clean. Talk about the three-dimensional shapes to be found in decorations and look for cylinders, cones, pyramids, spheres, cubes and cuboids. Look at those decorations which can be folded flat or taken apart in order to make storage easier.

Twelfth Night party

What you need
Mince pies or fairy cakes on two plates, a dried pea, a dried bean.

What to do
In some parts of the country people hold a Twelfth Night party, with a Twelfth Night cake. Inside this cake a dried pea and a dried bean are hidden and the lucky boy or girl who finds one of these is crowned Twelfth Night King or Queen.

You could have a Twelfth Night party and elect a king and queen in a similar way, using mince pies or fairy cakes on two large plates; one for the boys and one for the girls. Place the bean under one of the cakes on the boys' plate and the pea under one of the cakes on the girls' plate. Whoever chooses that cake will reveal the pea or bean and be thus elected and crowned.

Saraswati Puja

This is a Hindu festival celebrated in January or February on the day of *Basanta Panchami*. 'Basanta' means the 'season which follows winter' and 'Panchami' means 'the fifth day'. In this case, it is the fifth day after the new moon. The day of *Basanta Panchami* is kept as a day of worship of the goddess Saraswati, but the customs and celebrations are not the same all over India.

The season of *Basanta* begins on this day and usually at this time the fields are bright with yellow mustard flowers. This yellow colour is also called 'basant' and is a special colour for this season.

Saraswati is the goddess of learning and the arts. 'Puja' means 'worship', either in the temple or home. In Indian homes, the image of the goddess is placed on a raised platform on this feast to be worshipped and the area in front is decorated with beautiful patterns called 'alpana'.

Finding out day

What you need
No special requirements.

What to do
Since Saraswati is the goddess of learning, highlight to the children the importance of books. Take them to the school library and talk about the books there. Show them how the library is arranged and try to find books about things which interest the children. Discuss the sorts of questions to which they want to know the answers and show them how, with the aid of the right book, they can get all the information they need. This is a good exercise for all the children, even if they cannot read yet.

Setting up a yellow corner

What you need
A table, display materials, yellow items.

What to do
The yellow colour or 'basant' is special to the season of *Basanta*, so set up a yellow corner in the classroom. Ask the children to bring in things from home of all the different shades of yellow, and talk about the many different shades of yellow to be found, from the palest primrose to dark mustards and yellow ochre. Make the display as interesting as you can by draping the area with yellow, flowered fabric and using different display levels and labelling and allow as many different objects, both natural and manufactured, as possible.

Alpana pattern monoprints

What you need
Powder paint or ready-mixed paint, rectangles of plain white paper, plastic-topped table or sheets of perspex.

What to do
Since painting with rice water may not be practical in your situation, create a monoprint from a plastic-topped table or sheet of perspex. Alpana patterns are drawn in powdered rice and water paste on to the floor using the ring finger of the right hand in front of the goddess' platform to make the area beautiful. Spread a small amount of paint evenly over the surface of the table or perspex sheet. Talk to the children about the kinds of swirling patterns that can be made with the ring finger. Let the children experiment with making patterns with their fingers in the paint. When they have made a pattern with which they are happy, take a piece of white paper and place it over the pattern. Gently smooth out the air bubbles and then lift off the paper carefully to reveal the monoprint. The children's monoprints can be displayed around a picture of Saraswati to look like the *alpana* floor patterns.

Chinese New Year

Chinese people follow an ancient solar/lunar calendar, so the Chinese New Year (Yuan Tan) falls on a different day each year determined by a new moon. This usually falls between mid-January and mid-February. It is the most important Chinese festival, lasting for 15 days and is celebrated by Chinese communities all over the world. Chinese New Year begins as a family celebration. Just before the new year, people clean their homes thoroughly to wash away any bad luck. They clean their kitchens especially to appease the kitchen god, who is believed to report on the home to the higher gods before the festival begins, and they make sweet-tasting cakes for him. Red good luck decorations are hung on windows and doors and many people place flowering branches, such as plum or peach blossom, in their houses. In the Chinese communities of big cities, flags, banners and lanterns decorate the streets. It is a time for new beginnings; new clothes are worn, debts are paid and quarrels or bad relationships are forgotten. Special foods, such as *jiaozi*, are also prepared. Jiaozi are white flour dumplings, some of which contain hidden coins. Children are given 'lucky money' envelopes, and coins are shaken from a 'money tree' (a decorated branch) to bring good fortune.

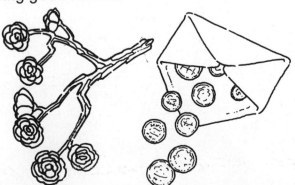

Each of the years is dedicated to a different animal on a twelve year cycle. There is a legend that twelve animals were chosen by the Chinese gods to represent the years, but the animals argued about who should be first. The gods resolved the matter by arranging a race across a big river, where the animal who won would be the first. The ox was winning, but the clever rat jumped on to his back to keep up and just at the last moment, as they approached the river bank, he jumped off and won the race. All the other animals followed each other out of the water in sequence from the rat; the ox, the tiger, the hare (or rabbit), the dragon, the snake, the horse, the ram (or sheep), the monkey, the rooster, the dog and the pig.

The animal for 1994 is the dog, so the animal for 1995 will be the pig. The pig is the last animal in the sequence so the cycle will be back to the beginning for the year after that, with the rat.

Kitchen-god cakes

What you need
Paper cake-cases, spoon, saucepan.
Ingredients
Rice Krispies, cooking chocolate, honey.

What to do
Melt the chocolate in a saucepan and stir in the Rice Krispies, till they have a good coating of chocolate. Spoon the mixture out into small cake-cases and leave to cool and harden. Drop a blob of honey on to the top of each cake to complete. Let the children help you with as much of each stage as you feel will be safe.

Good luck scrolls and New Year cards

What you need
Sheets of red A4 paper, gold crayons or felt-tipped pens, collage materials, gold foil, paper straws, scissors, adhesive.

What to do
Each child needs a piece of red A4 paper which can be folded to make a card or decorated and then hung as a scroll. the Chinese decorate their cards and scrolls with lions, dragons, peach blossom or kumquats (orange-like citrus fruits): symbols of good luck, happiness, long life, prosperity and good fortune. The children can design their own cards using some of these symbols and use the gold pens or crayons, gold paper and other collage materials to decorate them. To hang the scrolls, curl over the top and bottom of each scroll and stick it on to a paper straw.

Lucky money envelopes

What you need
Ordinary envelopes, sheets of red paper cut to the same size as the envelopes, gold wax crayons, a selection of coins.

What to do
Give each child a sheet of the red paper and show them how to make rubbings of the coins by placing a coin underneath the paper, feeling where the coin is and then rubbing gently over the surface with a gold wax crayon to create the rubbing. (The children may need to practise this a few times first with white paper and crayons.) When the children have made the patterns of coin rubbings on the red paper these can be stuck on to the fronts of ordinary envelopes to make 'lucky money' envelopes. The older children can experiment with making their own envelopes as well, if they wish. If necessary, show them how to fold a square of paper into thirds and staple two of the short edges or how to fold in and stick the corners of a square.

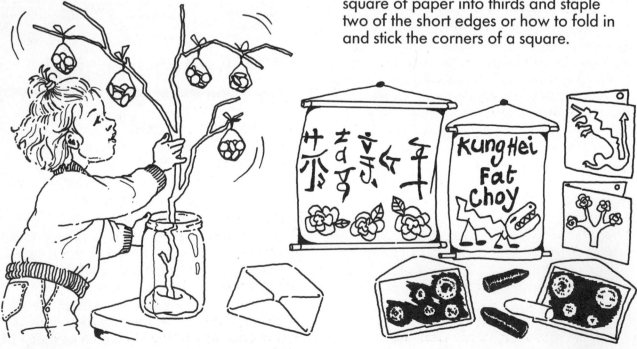

Chinese dragon puppet

What you need
Hinged plastic take-away burger containers, scraps of material, sequins, plastic bottle tops, pipe cleaners, glitter, adhesive, scissors, cardboard.

What to do
Let the children decorate the hinged burger boxes to look like dragons' heads by sticking two large bottle tops on the top of each lid, opposite the hinge, for the nostrils and cutting out two large eyes from card and folding these along their bottom edges to enable them to be stuck to the lid just behind the nostrils. Then each child can choose a piece of patterned material and stick this, with adult help, all around the top of the lid just behind the cardboard eyes. This is for the dragon's neck and to hide the puppeteer's hand. The children can now cut out some strips of sharp pointed teeth from paper for the dragon's mouth and decorate the dragon's head with sequins and glitter. Let them add streamers of paper or material by sticking them to the dragon's neck, which will further help to hide the hand.

When the dragons have been suitably decorated, show the children how to take hold of the hinged side of the dragon's head, making sure that their arms are covered by the material. By holding the hinged side carefully, and gently pressing the top and the bottom of the box, the dragon will be able to snap its jaws.

Money tree

What you need
Small branch of a tree, plastic plant pot, large lump of Plasticine, gold (spray) paint, small bags of foil-covered chocolate money.

What to do
Take the small branch and paint it gold. Spray paint should always be used in a well-ventilated area. Leave the branch to dry and then fix it in the plant pot, making sure it is quite secure by pressing it into the lump of Plasticine. Now you can hang the bags of foil-covered chocolate money on the branches to complete the tree. The children can take it in turns to shake the money tree. The children can take it in turns to shake the money tree. If a bag of coins falls off while the tree is being shaken the child gets to keep it. Make sure each child has a turn and have some coins in reserve, just in case any of the children have difficulty in shaking the bags of coins off.

Candlemas

This is a Christian festival which celebrates the presentation of Jesus Christ in the temple, when a holy man called Simeon spoke of him as, 'A light to lighten the Gentiles' (Luke 2:32). Jesus Christ is known as the 'Light of the world'. The festival falls on 2 February and the candles which are to be used in the church for the following year are blessed. In some places, blessed candles are given to the congregation.

Visit church

What you need
Contact with a church.

What to do
Try to arrange a visit to a local church. The minister may be willing to talk to the children and show them how the candles are blessed. Perhaps they could be given tiny white candles such as are used for birthday cakes. Take this opportunity to look around the church and show the children the altar, the decorations, the places where the congregation or the choir sit, the organ and so on. Perhaps children who are members of a Christian church could show the others round.

The idea of Jesus being a 'light for the world' is a difficult concept for this age group, but you could fruitfully discuss with the children which people in their lives make them happy or make them feel secure. Although the youngest will speak for themselves alone, as they mature children in this age group can be encouraged to listen to others' ideas and to feel that their own observations and feelings are valued.

Paper candles

What you need
White paper, adhesive, gold or silver foil, orange tissue paper, small plastic tubs, dried flowers (optional).

What to do
Cut the paper into rectangular strips (about 10cm x 25cm). Help the children to roll them along their length, securing the ends with adhesive. The children should then tear rough pieces of orange tissue paper for flames. Show them how to twist one end and dip this in adhesive and stick it in one end of the paper candle. Then stick a foil flame shape on to the tissue too.

Each child should then put a layer of adhesive into the bottom of a small white plastic tub and stand his or her candle in the centre, and then push some dried leaves, flowers or twigs into the adhesive around it for decoration. Display these against foil to brighten a February afternoon.

Setsubun

'Setsubun' (or the Japanese Bean Festival) actually means 'change of season' and is a festival to mark the last day of winter and the beginning of spring. It is held on 3 or 4 February and is celebrated in homes, in temples and in the streets. There is a custom of scattering roast beans in homes and on the streets to drive away devils. The children are given beans also, one for each year of their lives plus one for the future. The significance of the bean scattering is that it is a reminder that evil things are in the past and this a new start with the spring season.

Bean collage

What you need
An assortment of dried beans (different colours and sizes), adhesive, 12cm circles of natural coloured card, woodchip paper or hessian or cork tiles for display.

What to do
Help the children to count out their age plus one in each type of bean. Include large beans like butter beans and unusual colours like red kidney beans. Without using adhesive at this stage, help each child to lay out a design with the beans on a card circle. Some children may want help to lay out a repeating pattern, while others may want to make a face, for example. Encourage them to count their beans as they work. To fix the design, take off the beans and sort them into sets again and then spread adhesive over the surface of the card. The children can now repeat their designs into the adhesive.

Mount the cards, edges touching, on a background of woodchip wallpaper, hessian or cork.

Tu b'Shevat

Tu b'shevat is an Israeli spring tree planting festival which celebrates the end of winter. It takes place in January or February and falls on the fifteenth day of the Hebrew month of Shevat. Trees are associated with new and continuing life and it is customary in Israel, when a boy is born, to plant a cedar tree and when a girl is born, a cypress tree. This festival celebrates the importance of trees and children to the nation. On this day, the children sometimes parade through the streets with gardening tools, plant trees and then go on to general celebrations. It is a hopeful and happy time.

Growing fruit trees

What you need
Assorted fruit, plates, knives (for adult use), small plant pots, seed compost, old spoons, newspaper, card, lolly sticks.

What to do
Tree planting is one of the special activities of this festival and fruit trees are particularly important in the Israeli economy.

Cut up and collect the seeds from as many types of fruit as possible. Use the opportunity to observe and discuss with the children the different shapes, smells, textures and, of course, tastes. Help the children to make labels in appropriate fruit shapes using card and lolly sticks. Be aware of the risks of food allergies, particularly to oranges, strawberries and tomatoes. Always send a letter to parents before any 'tasting' activity, seeking information on any allergies and so on.

Moisten the compost beforehand and then show the children how to plant all the seeds at the same depth in the plant pots. Put them in a cool place to germinate. They will take different time periods to germinate, from a few days to years for a coconut plant. As a general rule, trees that live naturally in your country should germinate easily enough. Others from abroad may need different temperatures and moisture conditions. Encourage the children to observe the conditions carefully as the plants germinate and introduce them to the idea that plants generally need water and sunlight to grow by leaving one or two of the pots dry or in the dark. However, for children of this age, it may be wise to ensure the success of as many seeds as possible so that they can have the thrill of seeing their plants grow and develop. Growing trees is a worthwhile, if long-term, activity. You may be able to arrange for the children to take their trees with them through the different classes as many trees will grow well in tubs for many years.

Planting out your trees

What you need
Tree saplings (perhaps seeded in the children's gardens, or purchased from a nursery), garden tools, old washing-up liquid bottle; waterproof black felt-tipped pen.

What to do
Go for a walk with the children around the outside of your building to see if there is a suitable place to plant trees. You will need to find out what conditions are most suitable for the species you have. If you have chosen trees with widely differing needs you may like to consider planting them in containers. Dwarf conifers and very young large species will do well in containers, if properly husbanded. Also, this could be one answer to potential vandalism, as containers can be moved into more protected areas when the building is closed.

Show the children the different parts of the trees and explain the trees' needs. Let the children do the actual planting, if possible, splitting up the jobs for larger groups; someone to dig the hole, someone else to carry the water, another to cover up the roots and so on.

Finally, label the trees and establish a daily care routine. Make weatherproof labels for the trees from old washing-up liquid bottles as shown below.

Tree planting parade

What you need
Garden tools.

What to do
To enjoy the previous tree planting activity in the spirit of Tu b'Shevat, include a parade around your building with the children carrying the tools. Encourage them to clap and cheer as each tree is planted. You could sing the following song to the tune of 'Here we go round the mulberry bush'.

> We're going to plant some trees today,
> Trees today, trees today,
> We're going to plant some trees today,
> All on a happy morning.

Fruit and veg shop

What you need
Plastic or modelling clay fruit and vegetables, small containers, a table, corrugated card or a large cardboard box.

What to do
To follow up the exploration of fruit, make a small fruit and vegetable shop in a corner of the classroom. Make some fruit with the children's help using self-hardening clay, playdough, baked flour and water pastry or paper and let them sort these into sets to display. Encourage the children to use their experiences of real fruit to sell their products: 'These apples are really crisp and juicy!' You may be able to visit a local fruit shop to see how it is organised and take in the delicious smells and colourful sights.

Teng Chieh

Teng Chieh, the Chinese Lantern Festival, comes at the end of the Chinese New Year celebrations, two weeks after the festival of Yuan Tan, and is characterised by lanterns to represent the coming light of spring and the end of winter. The lanterns are made from a variety of materials and are decorated with the traditional symbols of the lion, the fish and the tiger. The lanterns are carried in procession, hung in shops and, in some villages, are hung from a central pole in a tent shape. The high spot of the festival is the 'Lion dance' which is performed in the street. The lion is sometimes over 30 metres long and has a highly decorated head and its body is made from bamboo cane covered in bright silk. Many people are involved in carrying it and performing the ritualistic twisting dance. People carry lanterns along the lion's route and music and fireworks add to the festive air.

The lion

What you need
Assorted cardboard boxes, rubber-solution adhesive, small card cylinders, shiny scrap materials (including foil, paint, red and gold glitter), small PE hoops, a long length of decorated, coloured lining material, staple gun.

What to do
To make a Chinese lion's head, use a strong, but light, cuboid box, large enough to cover the top half of a child's torso. Fix a light-weight box to the front as a snout and hinge a similar box to the underside of this with sticky tape. Try the head on an average-sized child and cut out a large rectangular 'vision' space above the dragon's snout. The child will be able to support such a light structure with his or her hands under the front or sides.

With the children's help, add features such as eyes (using the card cylinders), nostrils, teeth and mane using light scrap materials and paint the whole head in the colours of the children's choice. To give a traditional Chinese feel use reds and add lots of gold glitter.

To make the skirt of the lion, first let the children decorate the lining fabric, laying it on a flat surface to work on it. They can use sponge-printing or brushed paint lines. Let them add gold or red glitter for sparkle.

However long your fabric is, use one PE hoop for each metre, laying the fabric over each one evenly and fixing it in position with a staple gun. Leave 1m of fabric at the end to staple and tape to the back of the lion's head.

To operate the lion, one child holds the head and one child holds each of the hoops.

The lion dance

What you need
PE hoops, Chinese lion costume, small hand bells, Indian bells, small cymbals, maracas.

What to do
Help the children to sort themselves into groups of about six and ask them to make lines with each child holding the waist of the one in front. Let them try moving together in a line, following the speed of the leader. It is best to move at a slow pace at this proximity. Using PE hoops round their waists, with each child holding the front of his or her hoop and the back of the one in front, ask the children to try twisting and turning movements from side to side, then dipping and bending. Next ask the children to try to 'Follow-my-leader', with each child holding up the hoop in a vertical position and watching carefully the movements of the child in front.

Now let the groups of children take turns to do their dance with the lion costume. First discuss where they will move; for example, round the hall twice, across the hall once and in a circle once.

At a separate time work out a musical accompaniment of bells, cymbals and maracas, which the children think best illustrates the fierce lion's dance. They may decide that the cymbals should clash when the head is shaken, the maracas should shake to the speed of the feet, or the bells shake when the lion moves in a circle.

Finally, you can put the lion dance and the music together, letting all the children have a go at each activity. Perhaps they could perform the ensemble for another class.

It may be possible for you to arrange for a Chinese dance troupe to come to school to perform the 'Lion dance' for the school. Local Chinese business people or your local arts council may be able to provide a contact.

String lanterns

What you need
Brightly coloured thick string, PVA adhesive, shallow container, Plasticine, round balloons, ribbon, saucers, candles.

What to do
For each lantern, blow up a balloon quite fully and tie the end. Cut the string into 30cm lengths and put the adhesive in a shallow container. The pieces of string can then be laid in the adhesive as they are needed. To make the balloons easier to handle, you will need to fix them firmly into lumps of Plasticine and press the bases flat.

Applying the string to the balloon is quite difficult and messy and will need an adult to help, by holding the balloon. Show the children how to take one piece of string at a time and dip its full length into the adhesive and then place it over the balloon in any position. They should add one piece of string at a time, putting each one on in a different direction until the balloon is covered with a network, leaving a hole near the Plasticine base of about 8cm in diameter. Let the adhesive dry thoroughly for a couple of days and then pop the balloons and gently pull away the bits from inside the string network.

You can tie ribbon to the hole end and hang the lantern from a carrying stick or place the string cage over a candle on a saucer. This, of course, can be lit at your discretion.

St Valentine's Day

Valentine was a Christian Bishop of Rome in the third century AD and was reputedly put to death for his beliefs on the Eve of Lupercalia. Lupercalia was an Ancient Roman festival of the god Pan, in which part of the festivities included a pairing game for young men and women. Their names were put in a box, shaken up and then drawn out in pairs as token sweethearts. Legend has it that Valentine fell in love with his gaoler's daughter and as he was led to his execution he left her a love note signed, 'Your Valentine'. This story has led to the growth of the annual festival of lovers on 14 February when anonymous love notes are sent bearing the traditional symbols of hearts, lovers' posies and sentimental verses. The festival has now become widely commercialised and cards are produced to be sent to families and sweethearts. Country folklore in England says that on this day in early spring, even the birds find their mates.

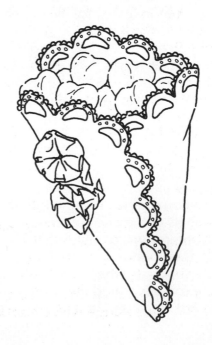

Fondant hearts

What you need
Ready-made white fondant icing, natural red food colouring, natural food flavouring, small heart-shaped pastry cutter, icing sugar, white doilies, rubber-solution glue, pink tissue paper circles.

What to do

The sweets
To colour the icing pink or red, add a tiny drop of colouring to a kneaded lump of the fondant icing and continue to knead until the colour is distributed as you like it. This need not be even as streaked colour gives a marbeled effect. Add the flavouring at this time too. The children can help with this kneading. Next divide the icing into manageable lumps, one for each child, and let them roll it out on a board dusted with icing sugar to prevent it sticking. Let them experiment with the thickness of the icing and the heart cutter, as too thin a shape could be difficult to handle, even when dry. A small, thick heart is the best product. Put each child's sweets on a named piece of paper to dry out in a cool place.

The packet
Show the children how to fold a doily almost in half and then twist it into a cone shape, securing the edge with a little adhesive. Make a flower decoration by twisting two circles of tissue into a flower shape and teasing out the petals, before fixing it to the joined edge with a spot of adhesive.

Valentine cards

What you need
White card, gold and red foil, gold or red plastic ribbon, small white doily, adhesive.

What to do
Cut out a number of each of three heart shapes; large white ones, medium gold ones and small red ones. Help the children each to fold a doily in half and then into a triangular fan or frill shape and stick this to a white heart about 5cm down from where the curves meet. They should then stick a gold heart in an equidistant position over this and finally a red heart on top of the gold. Make some loops of red or gold ribbon and show the children how to tape one to the reverse of each heart card. Any message can be written on the back for the youngest children, while children who have started writing for themselves can write their messages on small pieces of paper which can be stuck in position.

Shiva Ratri

Shiva is one of the three most important Hindu gods; the others being Brahma and Vishnu. Shiva is referred to as the 'King of Dancers' or as 'Nataraja' (Lord of the Dance) and, because of this, dancing is particularly associated with the festival of Shiva Ratri. In India, dance-drama is often used to tell the stories and legends of the Hindu gods and this helps people to understand their religion.

This festival usually takes place in February, but people do not need a reason to enjoy dancing which usually happens when people feel happy and able to respond to music. If there is someone in your community who can perform some of these dance-dramas, arrange for them to come into school and share their knowledge and art. This could lead to a performance by the children with costumes and masks.

Moving to music

What you need
Recording of Indian music, tape recorder.

What to do
Take the children into a large space and play some suitable Indian music. Recordings of world music are available from your local music library or parents may have suitable recordings. Talk to the children about the ways in which we can move. Start off with the children moving their hands and arms in time to the music. Encourage them to explore all the space around their bodies, reaching high up into the air and low down to the ground, and into the space in between, in front of and behind them. Give them plenty of practice in this and then include head movements, telling the children to focus their eyes slowly in different directions to make them turn their heads. When the children are ready you can combine all these actions to create a simple sequence of movements. Remember to emphasise the different levels of high, medium and low and encourage twists and turns of the body to face in different directions.

Mardi Gras or Shrove Tuesday

The day before the Christian season of Lent begins was originally called Shrove Tuesday, because on that day the Shriving bell rang calling everyone to church to be 'shriven', that is to confess their sins before beginning the time of preparation for Easter. Celebrating Lent also meant fasting — not eating any food on certain days and not eating certain foods on any days. Fasting clears the mind and body to prepare for the rites of the festival and allows for religious devotion and self-sacrifice. Eggs, meat and milk and rich, buttery dishes were the main foods to be avoided. All these kinds of foods had to be used up before Lent began, so the day became known as 'Fat Tuesday' or 'Mardi Gras'. One way of using up these foods was to make pancakes, so the day is also known as 'Pancake Day'. In some countries, the people hold colourful and noisy parades called 'carnivals'. This comes from the Latin words 'carnem levare' which mean 'to put away flesh', or 'to not eat meat'.

Making pancakes

What you need
Sieve, bowl, wooden spoon, frying pan, spatula.
Ingredients
(for 12 pancakes)
100g (4oz) plain flour
2 eggs
300ml (½ pint) milk
a pinch of salt
1 tbsp oil
1 tbsp white vegetable fat

What to do
The children will enjoy mixing the ingredients and older ones can help you to measure out the quantities.

Sieve the salt and flour into a bowl and make a small hollow in the middle. Crack the eggs into the hollow and slowly add half the milk. Stir the mixture with a wooden spoon to get rid of the lumps. Keep mixing until it is quite smooth, and then add the rest of the milk. Just before the pancakes are to be cooked stir in the oil. Melt just enough fat to grease the pan and heat it until it is very hot. (Remember to emphasise safety when working with young children and keep them well away from the hot fat.) Put two tablespoons of the mixture to cover the bottom of the pan. Cook the pancake on a medium heat until the underside is brown (you can check this by gently lifting the pancake with a spatula), then turn it over. If you toss it make sure you catch it in the pan. You can keep the cooked pancakes warm by putting them between two plates over a pan of simmering water. The children will not be able to participate in the cooking, but they will enjoy seeing the pancakes being tossed and will also enjoy eating the results afterwards.

To give the children a chance to toss pancakes, make paper ones by sticking three large-sized circles of paper together and let the children toss these instead. Circular bats or racquets can be used in place of frying pans.

Lenten calendars

What you need
A large piece of paper, black felt-tipped pen, colouring materials.

What to do
From France comes the tradition of making a Lenten calendar which looks like a nun. Make a large drawing of the nun as shown for the children to colour and decorate. The nun has to have seven feet, one for each week of Lent. As each week passes, one of the feet is tucked back under the nun's habit. The nun doesn't have a mouth to remind the children that Lent is a time of fasting.

Carnival masks

What you need
Basic cardboard mask shapes, paper plates, feathers, sequins, glitter, coloured activity paper, coloured foil, raffia, adhesive, scissors, thin elastic or pieces of garden cane.

What to do
Tell the children that when carnivals take place people often dress in fantastic costumes and wear masks so that no one knows who they are.

The children can decorate the basic mask shapes using feathers or sequins. Fringed paper strips can be used to decorate the eye holes, and noses, ears or beaks can be added by folding paper triangle or diamond shapes and sticking these in place.

The paper plates can be decorated in lots of different ways using similar materials. Let the children experiment by adding strips of foil, material or raffia for hair. The masks can be worn by threading two loops of elastic through holes at the side to wind around the ears, or a piece of garden cane can be taped to one side and the mask can be held up to cover the face as required. Once the masks have been made, the children can dress up and, wearing their masks, have a grand carnival parade.

The pancake

What you need
A version of the story of the runaway pancake.

What to do
Read or tell the story of the pancake who ran away and was chased by the cook, and a variety of other characters, until he came to a river and accepted a lift from a greedy wolf who ate him up. You may recognise this story as a European retelling of 'The gingerbread man'. Also say this poem:

Mix a pancake, stir a pancake,
Pop it in the pan.
Fry a pancake, toss a pancake,
Catch it if you can.

St David's Day

St David is the patron saint of Wales and his feast day is 1 March. Sainthood is a status given by those on Earth to individuals who have achieved a superior level of holiness and who have done great deeds in the service of the faith. David was an early Christian churchman who preached the Gospel and lived in the south west of Wales (where there is now a cathedral city named after him, St David's). Little is known about him except that he founded many churches and monasteries and helped to spread Christianity. On his feast day, the people of Wales celebrate their national identity with a cultural festival of song and music and they wear the national symbols of the daffodil or the leek.

A poetry reading

What you need
A selection of the children's favourite poems, any posters illustrating the poetry, daffodils, leeks, a Welsh flag, pre-recorded music (optional).

What to do
The Welsh people make St David's Day the starting point for such cultural events as poetry readings and musical performances. The Welsh people have always made a national pastime of their culture and value its expression highly.

Explain this to the children and then let them help you to create a Welsh festival corner with a Welsh flag, a vase of daffodils and/or some leeks on display with a poetry poster and then have a short poetry reading or speaking session. One of the children may have a doll dressed in Welsh national costume which he or she could bring in to school.

Lend the air of performance to each reading, encouraging the children to listen appreciatively and applaud or otherwise praise everyone's efforts.

You could include music in the event, either using a selection on audio tape with headphones available or as a performance, by individual children or small groups.

The weather in Wales

What you need
A television.

What to do
St David is the Welsh patron saint. As Wales is part of the British Isles the children need an opportunity to see where it is in relation to where they live. Watch one of the national weather forecasts on 1 March (or pre-record one on video to use at a convenient time) and point out to the children where Wales is in relation to their home town or village. Ask the children to note what the weather is like in Wales and later compare it with the weather in your area. Ask any children who have been on holiday to Wales what they remember about the country. With older children, watch the weather forecast everyday for a week and record the weather in Wales and at home daily, so that at the end of the week you can compare the two areas. If you live in Wales, not only can you find out where Wales is in the British Isles, but you can compare your weather with that of England, Scotland or Ireland.

Purim

Purim is a Jewish festival which celebrates how the Jewish people living in Persia were saved from death by Queen Esther. An official named Haman wanted all the Jews killed, and he arranged for dice to be used to decide when it should be done. Haman intended to start by hanging Queen Esther's uncle, Mordecai, but because of pleas by Esther to the king, Ahasuerus, all the Jews were saved and Haman was hanged on his own gallows. Purim gets its name from the Hebrew word '*pur*' which means 'dice' or 'lots' and is a day of rejoicing. The story of Esther is read from a special scroll called the '*megillah*', and the children are encouraged to make as much noise as they can whenever the name of the villain, Haman, is read. They shake 'graggars' and other noise-making instruments. Purim is a great time of celebration in Jewish communities, with music, plays and carnivals. It is a time for giving and receiving presents, and also a time for feasting. One of the favourite things to eat is '*Haman-tashen*', known as 'Haman's hats'. These are three cornered pastries filled with raisins and poppy seeds to represent the blackness of Haman's heart.

Haman-tashen

What you need
Bowl, pastry board, baking tray, round-ended knife.
Ingredients
For the pastry:
250g (8oz) plain flour
125g (4oz) lard
45ml (1tbsp) water (approximately)
pinch of salt
   For the filling you can use mincemeat, or raisins mixed with a little honey to bind them together. (Poppy seeds are not really popular with young children.)

What to do
Mix the flour and lard and a pinch of salt together till you get a crumbly texture, and then add the water and knead the mixture until smooth. Roll out the pastry and cut it into triangular shapes. Place a little of the filling in the centre of each shape and turn up the edges and pinch the corners to hold in the filling. Let the children help with as much of this as possible. Put the *Hamen-tashen* on a baking tray and into an oven at 220°C/ 425°F or Gas Mark 7 to cook for 20–25 minutes.

Make a graggar

What you need
Tin cans with replaceable lids, yoghurt cartons, paper plates, paints, crayons, felt-tipped pens, dried peas or beans, sticky tape.

What to do
If you decide to use the lidded tins, simply put some of the dried peas inside and tape the lid firmly so that the peas do not escape when it is being shaken.

Alternatively, take two yoghurt pots and put some of the peas or beans in one of them and put the other pot rim to rim with the first one, and tape them together. Younger children will need help with this and they can be encouraged to work with a partner, one to hold the pots together while the other sticks the tape round. When the containers are filled and taped securely, let the children decorate the outside with paints, coloured paper and foil.

Act the story of Esther

What you need
A version of the story of Esther, simple props for role-play such as crowns, cloaks and chairs.

What to do
First, read or tell the story of Esther (given in the Old Testament 'Book of Esther') to the children and talk about the characters. Discuss the way King Ahasuerus and Queen Esther might have walked and talked. Discuss the wicked Haman and what he might have been like, and finally talk about Mordecai and the way he would have behaved. The children could try walking and moving in the way of each of the characters as you read the story. With a few props, such as cloaks, crowns and hats, some of the children could act out the story of Esther as you read it, with the other children shaking their graggers each time the name of Haman is mentioned.

Purim songs and dancing

What you need
Recording of Purim songs and/or Israeli music, such as *Hebrew Festival Songs* by I. Camissar and M. Black (Maxsound Leeds Limited), tape recorder.

What to do
Purim is a time of dancing. A suitable tape, which contains some of the Purim songs, is *Hebrew Festival Songs* by Ian Camissar and Marcelle Black. The children can use these tunes and songs for rhythmic clapping games or you can structure their movements and incorporate sidesteps and turns as appropriate. Some of the songs are in English and the children may enjoy learning the simple ones so that they can sing along as the music plays. The younger children could skip freely to the music, on their own or with partners.

In Israel, all the children take part in fancy dress parties and parades, so you could round off the festivities with a fancy dress parade and a party complete with *Haman-tashen* and any other sweets of your choice.

Holi

Holi is a Hindu spring festival of new beginnings and harvest. The barley and wheat crops are gathered in accompanied by processions and dancing. It is a festival of fire and water, mirth and gaiety, when bonfires are lit to burn the rubbish of the past and welcome the future with optimism. The festival falls in March or April when the dry season begins and the fires and water help to purify the land.

The festival is named after a woman called Holika. According to a Hindu legend she tried to kill a brave boy, Prahlad, who remained faithful to the god Vishnu even when his own father maintained that he himself was the god to be worshipped.

At many such seasonal changes an element of misrule has crept into the proceedings and people are allowed to be rude to those who would normally command their respect. The custom during Holi is for people to run through the villages banging on doors and windows and throwing coloured water and paint at their friends and neighbours.

Swirling powder patterns

What you need
Rubber-solution adhesive, water in a plant-spray container, powder paint in assorted 'fire' colours, strong white cartridge paper, glue spreaders, large circles of fire-coloured paper (optional).

What to do
One of the fun misrule activities during Holi is the throwing of coloured powder and water at passers-by.

Cut the paper into circles and, using glue spreaders or old pencils, let the children dribble rubber-solution adhesive all over the paper in a swirling network of thin lines. Let the adhesive dry thoroughly; this may take a couple of hours. Next take the plant-spray and spray water all over the surface of the paper and adhesive. Using fingerfuls, let the children sprinkle an assortment of powder paint colours over their paper circles to cover them completely and let this dry. Shake off the excess powder and gently peel off the adhesive to reveal the unpainted, white swirling patterns underneath. Children with good hand control will be able to do this, but care is needed not to smudge the white pattern with the now dry paint.

These patterns can be mounted on larger circles of fire-coloured paper and displayed as if they were bubbles rising to the surface of water.

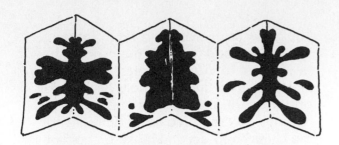

Concertina fire blobs

What you need
Strong coloured paper or card (white, yellow, orange or red), powder paint in assorted 'fire' colours, brushes.

What to do
Cut the paper into long strips (about 60cm x 10cm) and fold them into concertinas each with 6 parts; 3 pairs of pages as shown. Now open each concertina out to be painted. Using brushes, let the children dab one or more blobs of different coloured paint on to each of the surfaces and then fold up the concertinas to press all the surfaces together. Now help the children to open them out to see how the various fire colours have mixed to produce pairs of patterns. Display these to show the concertina-folds and joined end to end as a frieze.

Changing places

What you need
White A4 paper, felt-tipped pens or crayons.

What to do
For each child, fold a sheet of paper in half down its length and cut off the top third of the front. Keeping the paper folded, ask the children to draw their own heads to fill the spaces in the top third which is showing. Then tell them each to draw the rest of their body on the top sheet, dressed as they appear every day.

Discuss with them who they would like to be if they could change places for a day — would it be a TV character, a national hero, a friend or a parent? When they have decided individually, ask them to 'make this dream come true' by opening their papers and drawing their chosen character's body underneath their heads, so that, closed the sheet is the everyday self and, opened, each child becomes their alter ego!

You can assist the children by drawing faint pencil circles for head and body shapes of a shape and size that is easy to see and draw within.

Hola Mohalla

This is a Sikh festival, closely linked to the festival of Holi. Guru Gobind Singh thought that the festival of Holi was a little too irreverent and decided to set up his own celebrations based upon feats of strength and skill. He wanted to thank God for His bounty. The festival is based on strength because Sikhs feel that they should always be ready to defend their faith.

Things I can do

What you need
Large sheets of paper, black felt-tipped marker pen.

What to do
Children like nothing better than to be able to show how well they can do certain things. You may like to introduce an element of competition at this time to explain the idea behind Hola Mohalla.

The Sikhs value skills and strength as God-given and feel that they should be developed to their full potential. During Hola Mohalla the Sikhs hold tests of skill and strength, but with fun and good humour. Decide on a list of activities for the children to do and make a chart of how many and/or which of the children can do these things. It is important to be supportive and sympathetic to those children who find difficulty in accomplishing these tasks and to encourage effort and the acquisition of skills. Make sure that you find something that each child can do and give praise and encouragement. The activities might include hopping, skipping, jumping, running, riding a bicycle, swimming or throwing and catching a ball. Make a chart for the children to fill in to keep a record of the skills they have and those they hope to acquire.

Many children belong to clubs and societies outside school and they may be learning special skills there, such as playing the piano, swimming or karate. Encourage them to talk about this to the others. Can they say whether they have to do any special exercises or wear special shoes or clothes? They may even be persuaded to give a demonstration of their skills to the others.

These children can do these things:					
5	🏃				
4	🏃	skip			
3	🏃	skip			jump
2	🏃	skip	hop	sing	jump
1	🏃	skip	hop	sing	jump
	run	skip	hop	sing	jump

St Patrick's Day

St Patrick is the patron saint of Ireland and he is remembered each year on 17 March. This festival is celebrated in many countries of the world, especially where there is a group of Irish people or their descendants living. Irish people wear a piece of a three-leaved plant called shamrock on this day to remind them that St Patrick used this plant to explain the Christian belief that God is three beings and one at the same time.

Another legend about St Patrick tells of how he managed to rid Ireland of snakes. There were many snakes and people were very frightened of them, so St Patrick is said to have made all the snakes follow him up to the top of a high cliff, from where he drove them down into the sea. Since when there have been no snakes seen in Ireland.

Why are plants green?

What you need
Shamrock, packet of mustard or cress seeds, any growing medium (cotton wool or blotting paper), water, shallow dishes.

What to do
Irish people often wear the colour green on St Patrick's Day and this is probably taken from the colour of the shamrock plant. Try to obtain some shamrock (or clover) and talk about it with the children.

Look at the leaves. Ask the children to suggest reasons for the leaves being that colour. Are leaves always green?

Take one of the shallow dishes and line it with a thin layer of moist growing medium. Sprinkle some of the seeds over the surface and leave this dish in a warm, sunny place. Do the same with a second dish, but this time place the dish in a warm, dark place. After a few days check to see what has happened. Ask the children to suggest reasons why the two sets of seedlings are different.

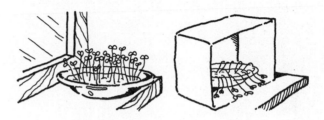

Snake movement

What you need
A large, empty indoor or outdoor space, suitable music such as 'Trust in me' from the soundtrack of the Walt Disney film of The Jungle Book.

What to do
Tell the children the story of St Patrick and the snakes. Discuss the way in which snakes move. Encourage the children to use their arms to suggest snake-like movements. Talk about wide and narrow shapes. How can the children make their bodies long and narrow? Talk about where snakes move and ask the children to suggest ways of moving across the floor like a snake. Talk about changes of direction and what might happen if two snakes met. A good piece of music to accompany this lesson might be, 'Trust in me' from the soundtrack of the Walt Disney film of The Jungle Book.

Interlocking snake

What you need
Cartridge paper, scissors, crayons or powder paint or ready-mixed paint or felt-tipped pens or collage materials.

What to do
To link with the story of St Patrick and the snakes make a huge snake mobile to trail all around the classroom. Each child can contribute by decorating one or more of the units which interlock to make its body.

For each unit of the snake's body, take a rectangle of cartridge paper, fold it down its length and draw on the shape shown below. The size of rectangle you choose and the number of children involved will determine the length of the finished snake.

The children may need help to cut out the shapes. Then they can open up the shapes and decorate both sides of them, using paint, crayons, felt-tipped pens or collage materials. The edges can be trimmed later if the collage materials overlap.

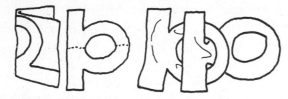

When all the shapes have been decorated, join them together by inserting the wide end of one shape into the loop of the previous one, thus making the body which can be as long as you wish. Finish off the snake by painting and adding the snake's head and display it by hanging it from the ceiling or draping it around the room.

Mothering Sunday

Mothering Sunday was originally a British Christian festival, celebrated on the fourth Sunday in Lent, the traditional fast before Easter. Easter is a moveable feast calculated on a lunar cycle and can occur in March or April. Mothering Sunday is the one day in Lent when people are allowed to break their fast and celebrate. This festival dates at least from the seventeenth century. People in outlying villages would take offerings to the mother church of the parish. Later it became the custom for apprentices and servant girls to be allowed a day off to go home to visit their own mothers to whom they gave cakes or small posies of flowers. Simnel cake was a rich fruit cake baked for this day, but often kept uneaten until Easter and the end of Lent.

Today the festival has developed into a more secular version — Mother's Day. Cards and flowers are sent widely and the focus of attention is the family and honouring the mother's role.

However, the role of the mother may be a sensitive issue for some children in your class, in which case discuss the validity of other female carers such as step-mothers, guardians, foster mums, or even grandmothers who take on full care. This is a day to celebrate the female role in parenting, but any such issues must be handled to suit your class.

Mother's Day card

What you need
Stiff white card, shiny silver 'mirror' card, assorted small pasta shapes or seeds or dried flowers or coloured tissue paper, black felt-tipped pen, adhesive, gold spray paint.

What to do
For each child, cut a piece of card 30cm x 12cm and fold it in half. Next cut an oval piece of the shiny silver card that will fit comfortably on the front of the folded card with a margin of about 2cm. Mark where the shiny card will be attached with a feint pencil line. The children can now decorate the corners of the card to look like an ornamented mirror, using any combination of the pasta or seeds. These are fixed on to a small bed of adhesive, which is allowed to dry thoroughly. if you wish, the fronts of the cards can now be sprayed with gold paint, but this should be done by an adult in a well-ventilated area. Alternatively, the gold paint can be omitted and the corners of the cards decorated with dried flowers and pasta shapes or the mirrors can be edged with small pieces of screwed-up tissue paper to represent tiny flowers. Finally, fix the silver mirror shapes to the centre of the cards and add a label underneath with the sentiment 'This is the best mum in the world.', 'You are wonderful.', 'Supermum' or whatever the children think is most suitable.

Mothers!

What you need
Paper, pens, children's tape recorder, blank tape.

What to do
Ask the children to draw pictures or bring in photographs of their mums. These can be shown to the group to inspire discussion. Talk about such topics as:
- why I love mum;
- mum's appearance;
- things mum does;
- ways I can help mum.

Record the discussions when the conversation is going well and allow the children to replay them. You could set up a small, intimate listening corner for one or two children. If possible, use a children's tape recorder, to allow the children to use the machine themselves to replay and review the conversations.

You could also make a class list of some of the suggestions, for example, of ways to help mum. For emergent readers include a visual clue. For example, for 'Tidy my room' add a small picture of some toys to the list.

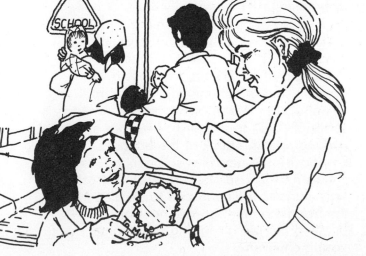

All Fool's or April Fool's Day

All Fool's Day is celebrated on 1 April. It is said to be linked to the fact that in France in 1564 it was decided to change the day on which the new year started, from 1 April to 1 January. Real gifts and messages were to be given on 1 January, but people decided to give joke gifts and messages on the day that had once been the start of the new year, that is 1 April. People still play tricks on each other and make jokes, but they are only allowed to do it up until midday. After that time if they play a joke on someone they will be the April Fool.

A jester's stick

What you need
Sheet of newspaper, tape, balloon, small spherical bells.

What you do
Talk about jesters and clowns. Discuss the clothes they wear and tell the children that sometimes a jester carries a stick. He uses this to chase people and when he catches them he will hit them with it. To prevent injury, traditionally the stick has an inflated pig's bladder on the end (or a balloon, today) with which the victim would be hit.

Instead of a pig's bladder, use a balloon and attach this to a rolled-up newspaper. Tie one or two small spherical bells to the end of the paper rod, nearest the neck of the balloon. Emphasise the need for safety if the children do chase each other and stress only parts of the body are to be hit, not the head. Remember too, balloons bursting can be a real fright for some young children.

A joke competition

What you need
No special requirements.

What to do
Most children know at least one joke and often they do not need much encouragement to tell it. It is as well to have a few jokes of your own ready to tell just to start the children off. Make a note of their best ones, and suggest that the children collect suitable jokes from home too. You can either record the children telling their jokes, using a tape recorder, for them to play back later, or you could make a joke book for them to illustrate, which they will enjoy reading in the book corner.

You can perhaps link this topic with a charity effort such as with 'Comic Relief Day', which takes place around this time. Think of crazy things which the children might like to do, such as a sponsored smile or a craziest face painting competition, perhaps with the incentive of raising money for a particular charity.

Hana Matsuri

Hana Matsuri is a Japanese flower festival held 1–8 April, which celebrates the birth of Buddha. In most Japanese Mahayana Buddhist homes an image of the infant Buddha is placed on a small stand decorated with flowers and placed outside a small temple. The flowers recall the flower-decked garden where the infant Buddha was born. For the first few days of the festival, the Japanese people go to look at the cherry blossom which blooms on the trees at this time. They regard the cherry blossom as a symbol of national pride and hope. On the eighth day of the festival, the day of the birth of Buddha, the children anoint the image with a fragrant tea (*amacha*) to remind them of the perfumed water provided by heavenly spirits for the Buddha's first bath in India.

You may like to compare the story of the birth of Buddha with the story of the birth of Christ. They are very different. In the same way that you might set up a Christmas crib scene, you might like to create a flower-decked corner where you can place an image of the infant Buddha, or a small doll to represent him.

Decorated branches

What you need
Bare branches of a suitable size, small circles of white or pink tissue paper, adhesive.

What to do
Show the children how to take a small circle of tissue paper and fold it in half, place the folded shape between the finger and thumb of one hand and with the fingers of the other hand make the folded tissue paper into a flower shape and twist the folded edge to hold the shape.

Encourage the children to make lots of these tissue paper twists and stick them on to bare branches to give the appearance of blossom. Place these in containers around the figure of Buddha.

Making branches bloom

What you need
Branches cut from flowering shrubs or trees in the garden, containers to display them in.

What to do
Cut branches from flowering garden shrubs and put them in water in a warm place. The heat will encourage the flowers to open much earlier than those outside. Talk about this with the children and keep a record of how long it takes the branches inside to flower, compared to those still on the bushes outside. Some flowering shrubs, such as *Forsythia*, may actually start to root in the water so encourage the children to look out for this and, if possible, plant these cuttings out in the school garden after flowering.

Passover

This is one of the oldest Jewish festivals. It is celebrated in the spring with an eight day family festival of thanksgiving. It is called *Pesach* in Hebrew and serves as a constant reminder of the Jews' deliverance from slavery in Egypt at the time of Moses and their journey to freedom in Irsael. 'Passover' means 'passing over' and the name recalls how God protected the Jews so that the ten plagues he sent passed over their homes and went to those of the Egyptians. They also remember how Moses parted the waters of the Red Sea to lead them to safety.

The Torah, the Jewish holy book, decrees that the story should be told to the children each year and this story is in the *Haggadah* (from the Hebrew 'to tell'), a book that provides guidance for the observance of the festival and contains songs and prayers of thanksgiving.

Before the festival begins the whole house is cleaned and a search made for any 'leaven' (yeast). The whole family gather together on the first night of the festival for a special meal called the *Seder*. They wear new clothes and there are candles and a cup of wine for each person and one for any unexpected guest. There are certain symbolic foods served on the '*Seder* Plate': the *matzoh* (unleavened bread) reminds the people of the bread made in haste as the Jews fled Egypt; parsley dipped in salt reminds them of the scanty food and the tears shed in Egypt; a roast shank of lamb represents the Paschal lamb, sacrificed in gratitude for their release; a roasted egg represents the Jews' new life; *maror*, a bitter herb (like horseradish) reminds them of the bitterness of slavery and *haroset* (a sweet of nuts and fruit) emphasises the sweetness of deliverance and freedom.

After the *kiddush* (or blessing) has been spoken, the youngest child present asks four questions of the father (head of the household) who, in his answers, reminds the family of the reasons for celebrating *Pesach*. Afterwards there are prayers and hymns at home, as well as at the Synagogue, to celebrate their deliverance from slavery and consequent freedom.

A family feast

What you need
A teaset.

What to do
Spring-clean the home corner and let the children select 'new clothes' from the dressing-up clothes. A waistcoat or skirt will suffice to transform a character.

Discuss with the children the reasons for the family feast at the beginning of the Passover festival and use toy food to represent the '*Seder* Plate'. Count how many 'family' members there are playing in the home corner and ask the children to work out the correct place settings, using quantity concepts such as, 'enough', 'not enough', 'plenty', 'how many?' and so on. Explore the use of space and shape on the table as you try to fit everything on. Would the plates fit better side by side if they were square?

To explore the dramatic possibilities, introduce a visitor to the home corner (yourself, for instance) and ask the children to show how their 'family' extends hospitality. For the Jews this is a joy and a duty.

Haroset

What you need
Grater, bowls, spoons.
Ingredients
(For about six portions.)
2 apples
½ cup chopped walnuts
2 tbsp apple juice
1 tbsp chopped dates and raisins
½ tsp cinnamon

What to do
This is a traditional dish served at Passover and is said to be a reminder of the mortar used by the Jewish slaves to build cities in Egypt for the Pharoah.

Core the apples and then grate them coarsely. Add the chopped nuts and fruit and the cinnamon and mix well. Finally, add the apple juice to the mixture and mix again. Serve in small bowls to be eaten straight away. For those who dislike the cinnamon, add a teaspoon of brown sugar instead.

The recipe for this dish varies and is sometimes made to a paste consistency. The bitter herbs are dipped into this before being eaten.

Moses and the Red Sea

What you need
Song about Moses to teach the children, e.g., 'How did Moses cross the Red Sea?' in *Junior Praise* (1986, Horrobin & Leavers), piano or guitar (optional).

What to do
Tell the children the story of how Moses led the people of Israel away from their captivity in Egypt (Exodus 7–14). Many resource books for example, have these stories in great detail; however, for youngest children it may be advisable to omit the details about the Angel of Death and the ten plagues and concentrate on the escape and the miraculous crossing of the Red Sea, when Moses commanded the waves to part and led the people safely to the other shore and freedom. The waves then closed on the following Egyptian army and drowned them.

Teach the children a song such as, 'How did Moses cross the Red Sea?' The tunes are simple and repetitive enough for the youngest children as well as being great fun to sing.

Act out the crossing of the Red Sea with three groups of children, with two groups pretending to be the waves and one the Israelites being led by Moses. Let the children try out the sweeping movements of the waves with outstretched arms and running steps and encourage the Israelite group to try huddling together to hurry in fear across the space between the two wave groups. Moses told the Israelites to trust in God and they became confident and walked with pride. Ask the children to try these different ways of walking. Let the groups change roles to get a feel for the whole story.

Hina Matsuri

This is the Japanese Doll or Peach Festival. It originated at a time when Japanese people believed that dolls could drive away evil spirits. Japanese families with daughters observe the Hina Doll Festival on 3 March. Towards the end of February they set out tiered stands covered with scarlet felt and an elaborate set of dolls is displayed. The dolls represent the Emperor, Empress, attendants and musicians in ancient dress. The Emperor and Empress are placed on the top shelves and ladies-in-waiting and their attendants are placed on lower shelves. On the bottom shelf are placed little musical instruments and miniature furniture, and peach blossom is placed all around. The families celebrate with a special meal of soup, fish and a diamond-shaped rice cake called *hishimochi* and they drink a rice wine called *shirozake*. It is the custom for Japanese parents to present their daughter with her Hina doll set at birth and for her to take it with her when she marries. Long ago in Japan, parents used to make paper dolls with their children's names written on them. They believed that if they rubbed the children's bodies with the paper dolls they would soak up all the illness that might come during the next year. The dolls were then taken to the nearest river and placed in it, in the hope that as they floated away they would take away all the diseases with them.

Japanese peg doll

What you need
Wooden clothes pegs, scraps of silk or shiny material, lengths of brightly coloured ribbon, sequins and glitter magazine pictures (optional).

What to do
Cut out squares of the shiny material large enough to wrap around the clothes peg. Help the children to place the squares down and fold up the bottom corner and then place the peg in the centre of the material and wrap the material over the peg to make the kimono. They should tie a length of ribbon around the middle of the peg to hold the kimono in place. A spot of adhesive on the back of the top of the peg will stick the top point of the material to the peg to prevent the kimono slipping off. Let the children draw the faces of the Emperor and Empress or cut out faces from magazine pictures and stick them on to the peg dolls. The kimonos can then be decorated using the sequins and glitter.

Clay dolls

What you need
Clay or self-hardening modelling medium (such as Newclay), paints and varnish.

What to do

The children will enjoy making their very own baby dolls. For very young children, the dolls can be as simple as a shaped lump of clay with eyes, nose and mouth pressed into the surface with a pointed implement. Older children can fashion limbs as well and include finer details such as hair and hands and feet. The clay dolls can be hardened and then painted and varnished. They can be used instead of the wooden pegs in the previous activity if you so wish.

Doll display

What you need

The children's favourite dolls.

What to do

Ask the children to bring in their favourite dolls to take part in their own Hina Festival. Set up a display of these in the classroom or entrance hall. As part of the festival, some of the children may like to talk about their dolls and tell the others when they got them, whether they have special names and what it is that makes them so special. There is no reason why this activity should be limited to girls, most boys have their own action figures and will be just as enthusiastic to talk about them. This will be a good opportunity to talk about things which are dear to you and the children, and about caring for other people's property. Explain that everything is special to someone and so people are sad if anything bad happens to something which they own. Discuss how the children would feel if they lost a favourite toy or if it was damaged. This may help them to realise the importance of looking after things.

Easter

Easter is the most important festival in the Christian church year. The name 'Easter' comes from the name of the Saxon goddess 'Eastre' or 'Eostre'. She was the goddess of the dawn and her spring festival was celebrated in April. Before the arrival of Christianity, people believed that the sun died in winter and was born again in spring, heralded by Eastre.

Eggs, the hare, and chicks are all symbols associated with Easter, since they remind us of new life in spring after winter. There are two sides to this festival. One reminds us of rebirth in nature, and the other reminds us of the death of Jesus Christ by crucifixion and the Christian belief in his resurrection on Easter Day, to bring new hope and life to those who believe in God.

As with most Christian festivals the date of Easter coincides with a former pagan festival. The first Easter took place during the Jewish Passover feast which is always celebrated at full moon, so to keep Easter Day on a Sunday, it was decided that Easter should always be celebrated on the Sunday following the first full moon after the spring equinox (21 March).

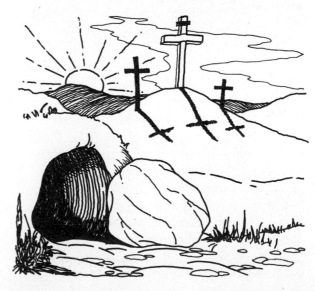

Make an Easter garden

What you need
A shallow tray, compost or soil, small pebbles or gravel, peg dolls or similar small figures (optional), shallow dish (optional), spring plants such as primroses or miniature daffodils. (If these plants are not available, you can grow cress, carrot tops and onion tops as the plants in your garden.)

What to do
Cover the bottom of the shallow tray with compost or soil and lay a path of pebbles or gravel. Let the children decide where the plants are to go. They will need to look after their garden and keep it watered. You could make space for a little pond by sinking a shallow dish into the surface of the soil and filling it with water. The addition of one or two small figures will make it more interesting.

You can vary this idea by making a garden with a large mound to represent the hill of Calvary. With the children's help, cover the mound with moss and at the bottom make a small hollow and place a large flat stone at the side. This is to represent Christ's tomb. Lay a path of gravel around the entrance. On top of the mound place three small crosses made from lollipop sticks or thin twigs, and halfway down the mound make a space for a small container for seasonal flowers. Make sure that you spray the moss regularly with water to keep it fresh.

Nature watch

What you need
A walk around the school grounds or neighbourhood.

What to do
Easter and spring are usually associated together in this country. During the weeks leading up to Easter, look for the changes in nature. Look for signs of the birds building nests, changes in the weather, fresh green shoots in the ground and on trees, creatures being born. Talk about spring-cleaning in the home and ways in which the children can help.

Easter egg hunt

What you need
Small chocolate eggs, basket for collecting the eggs.

What to do
Decide where the Easter egg hunt is to take place. It could be in the classroom or playground. Make sure you hide the eggs so that they are not too easy to find, and warn other staff that the egg hunt is taking place. Give the children a time limit and ask them to bring all the eggs they find to a central basket so that they can be shared out equally at the end.

Easter hat

What you need

Strips of green card, large plastic drink bottle, paints, crayons, felt-tipped pens, green tissue paper, small pieces of thin twig or art straws painted brown.

What to do

Give each child a strip of green card and tell them to decorate the strips with leaf shapes, cut from green tissue paper, and small pieces of thin twig or art straws painted brown. Cut pieces from the plastic bottle so that you have a number of arched strips. Each child should then draw a bird with outstretched wings, which can be stapled to the plastic strip. The other end of the plastic strip is stapled to the headband she or he has decorated and then this should be formed into a circlet to fit the child's head. As the children nod their heads, the birds will bob up and down.

This idea can be adapted to show a bee buzzing around a flower or a dragonfly flitting around a pond.

Easter card

What you need

Card or thick paper, crêpe paper, adhesive, shiny foil paper or paints or felt-tipped pens or crayons.

What to do

Fold a sheet of card or thick paper in half and cut out an egg shape, taking care not to cut along the fold. The children can decorate the fronts of their egg shapes by speckling paint on them with toothbrushes or by cutting strips of shiny foil paper and laying these in horizontal stripes to cover the egg shapes. Alternatively, patterns can be made with crayon in an all-over design or as wax-resist. When thoroughly dry, cut strips of crêpe paper about 2–3cm wide and long enough to go around the egg card and leave two ends long enough to be tied. Stick one of these ribbons across the middle of each egg card, front and back. A message may be written inside by the child or an older or adult scribe and then the crêpe paper can be tied in a bow to hold the card shut.

Baisakhi

The festival of Baisakhi marks the Sikh New Year and is celebrated on 13 April. It commemorates the occasion in 1699 when Guru Gobind Singh, the tenth leader, gathered all Sikhs together and introduced the *Khalsa*. This was the idea that all Sikhs should become part of a strong military brotherhood who would swear loyalty to their faith and promise to defend the weak. There is a special initiation ceremony during the festival for people who wish to become members of the *Khalsa* brotherhood. They drink a special kind of sugared water called *amrit*, and they adopt the five Ks:

Kesh — uncut hair and beard, a symbol of devotion to God;
Kanga — a comb which keeps the hair in place, is an indication of cleanliness;
Kara — a steel bracelet worn on the right wrist, symbolising the strength and unity of the Sikhs;
Kirpan — a short sword which is a reminder to defend the truth and the weak;
Kaccha — shorts which give greater freedom than the usual Indian clothing and symbolise modesty and restraint.

With the turban, these five items make up a uniform which all Sikhs wear. Before this ceremony there are two days of prayer and readings from the Sikh holy book, the Guru Granth Sahib. At the ceremony the congregation shares fruit and *Karah Prashad*, a mixture of flour, milk, ghee and sugar. After the ceremony, the congregation eats a vegetarian meal together in an adjoining room.

Special uniforms

What you need
A representative of a uniformed profession (optional).

What to do
Talk to the children about uniforms, the special clothes which help us to know the kinds of jobs people do. Try to identify those people in uniform who help us. Why do they need a uniform? Is it so that everyone will be able to recognise them, or maybe they need the special clothes for protection in their jobs, or so that they can be seen easily? Invite a representative from the police, fire brigade or ambulance service into school to talk about his or her job. Maybe one of the children has a father or mother

who is in one of the armed forces, or in another kind of organisation that has distinctive clothes or a uniform, such as the Guides, Scouts or even a church choir. Invite her or him into school to show the children the clothes he or she wears. If any members of a Sikh family are willing to come into school, they could actually show the children the elements of the *Khalsa* and talk about their significance. If they were willing to leave examples of the items in school you could set up a display, otherwise draw a large picture of a man wearing the five Ks. Label all the different parts and make cards the same which the children can match to the labels on the picture and hold in place with Blu-Tack.

As a follow-up to this, organise a mini topic on 'People who help us'. You may be able to arrange a visit to a fire station, or ask the local ambulance service if an ambulance could call at the school. The local police may also be able to arrange a visit by a patrol car or a police dog handler with his dog. One of the children may have a parent who is a nurse, or you may be able to talk to the person who delivers mail to school.

St George's Day

St George is the patron saint of England and 23 April is his special feast day. There is not a great deal known about St George, but the most commonly held belief is that he was a Roman soldier who was put to death by the emperor because he was a Christian. He is usually shown as being a brave knight on a white horse and there is a legend that he killed a fierce dragon and so saved a beautiful princess. His flag has a red cross on a white background and this was the flag which the Crusaders took with them as they rode into battle. On 23 April, you can see this flag flying over many public buildings in England.

Make a flag of St George

What you need
Rectangles of white paper, red paint, tightly rolled paper (for flag poles).

What to do
Draw a vertical and a horizontal line in pencil through the centre point of each sheet of white paper. This is to act as a guide for the children. Then let them paint over the lines with red paint. Leave the flags to dry and then attach them to flag poles made from tightly rolled paper.

Cotton reel dragon

What you need
Selection of plastic cotton reels, length of strong string, two yoghurt pots, lengths of tissue paper, green paint, coloured card, PVA adhesive, buttons (optional), coloured felt (optional).

What to do
Take the length of string and tie a knot in one end. Let the children thread the cotton reels on one by one until the dragon is as long as you want it. Now take the two yoghurt pots and make a hole in the bottom of one of them. The children can then thread the string through the hole and you can tie a knot in the string so that it holds all the reels together and secures the yoghurt pot as well. Now stick the second yoghurt pot rim to rim with the first one to complete the head. The dragon is now ready to be decorated by the children. They can paint it green and attach small triangles of green card to each cotton reel for its scaly back. They should paint the yoghurt pots with a mixture of paint and PVA adhesive. Let them use a different colour for the mouth and draw or stick buttons on for eyes. A felt forked tongue on the end of the second yoghurt pot and strips of tissue paper stuck on the tail end will add to the effect. The dragon can then be hung from the ceiling by fixing a loop of string to the head and tail.

Talk about heroes and heroines

What you need
Stories about heroes and heroines, such as 'David and Goliath' or 'Anne Frank'.

What to do
Look at other stories of bravery, and talk about what makes a hero. Is it just about fighting dragons or being a superhero. Ask the children to try and think of something they have done which was very brave, such as a visit to the dentist or going into hospital or being outside when it was thundering and lightning. Help them to write their story, with an adult helper as a scribe for the very youngest children, and call the story 'My brave deed'.

Eid-ul-Fitr

Muslims are people who follow the religion of Islam which is based on the teachings of the prophet Muhammad who lived about 1,400 years ago. He wanted people to believe in Allah. Part of their belief is the period of one month of fasting called 'Ramadan' (the ninth month of the Islamic calendar). It does not start on the same date each year. Islam uses the phases of the moon to measure its months, so Eid-ul-Fitr falls about eleven days earlier each time and so moves round the calendar. (Check the precise date in the current *Shap Calendar of Religious Festivals*.) During Ramadan Muslims have to get up before dawn to have their breakfast, and then they have nothing else to eat, neither food nor drink, from sunrise to sunset. During Ramadan Muslims attend the mosque and involve themselves in religious matters as much as they can.

On the last night of Ramadan, when a new moon is expected, the people will often crowd the streets looking for the sign that Ramadan is over. The first day of the new month is celebrated as Eid-ul-Fitr, the festival of fast breaking. People usually break the fast by eating a date. They go to the mosque at dawn and say special prayers and then they offer money to charity (*zakat-ul-fitr*). After this they will have a special breakfast and then families go to visit each other, wearing new or clean clothes. They often take gifts of sweets and sugared almonds in decorated boxes to give to friends and the children are given gifts of sweets, nuts and money. People often exchange Eid cards and wish each other '*Eid Mubarak*', or Happy Eid.

Children under the age of ten are not expected to fast, but to give the children the idea of fasting and what it might be like, you may be able to ask them if they would like to forego their mid-morning snack. Perhaps, with the help of their parents, they could contribute the money they would have spent on crisps or chocolate bars to a worthwhile cause. Highlight the needs of the people you are trying to help and stress the positive aspect of the children doing something themselves to help others. If this is not acceptable, you could ask the children to bring in unwanted toys for a bring and buy sale, again to raise money for charity. Link any charity effort to the giving of *zakat*.

Islamic patterns

What you need
Squared paper, coloured pencils or felt-tipped pens.

What to do
For many young children the idea of a repeating pattern is quite a difficult concept. Introduce the idea by giving the children pegboards and coloured plastic pegs. Set the pegs on the top row in a repeating sequence of, say, red, blue, red, blue and so on, and ask the children to copy the pattern on the row below. Once they have got the idea, give them squared paper and start them off by colouring the first few squares in a sequence, and then ask them to continue the pattern. After a little practice they should be able to start creating their own patterns. Older children can start to put circles or diagonal lines of different colours in the squares to make their patterns more intricate.

Decorated sweet box

What you need
Large rectangular plastic margarine tubs, scraps of coloured tissue paper, PVA adhesive, strips of lace or paper doilies.

What to do
Let the children tear or cut the tissue paper into irregularly shaped pieces. Tell them to turn their margarine tubs upside down and cover them by sticking the tissue paper pieces all over. Show them how to overlap the pieces to make sure that their tubs are covered completely.

They should cover the insides in the same way and 'varnish' the entire surface inside and out with a coating of thinned PVA adhesive. This will dry to a shiny finish. They can trim the rims of the tubs by sticking on strips of lace or the outer edges of paper doilies around it. Fill the finished box with sugared almonds or the sweets of your children's choice.

Eid cards

What you need
Thin card, coloured paper, foil, adhesive, felt-tipped pens or coloured crayons, scissors.

What you do
First, explain to the children that Eid cards open the opposite way to the cards we usually send because Muslims write from right to left. Also, the Islamic religion forbids making pictures of living things, but such things as flowers, repeated patterns, minarets or pictures of the new moon with the greeting 'Eid Mubarak' are acceptable. Discuss the sorts of things that the children might want to put on their cards and let them plan their designs. For younger children, a cut-out silver moon and a coloured card minaret on a contrasting coloured card is very effective.

May – August

Chapter two

The months of May, June, July and August are the summer months in the Northern hemisphere. In this section are included religious and secular festivals of great variety. Some celebrate the births of the founders of religions, while others celebrate family relationships or recognise the good qualities in certain members of the family. Do be aware of the child who comes from a one-parent family, for example, and try to include them in the activities in as sensitive a way as possible.

May Day

May Day celebrations are not as important today as they were in the past. For hundreds of years May Day was one of the most important days of the year when people celebrated the beginning of summer.

In many countries May Day is a secular (often politically-based) national holiday. In England there is a holiday on the nearest Monday to 1 May. Long ago, people walked in procession carrying branches of may (hawthorn) blossom. They would choose a tall young tree and strip off its lower branches, leaving just the top ones (to represent new life), and then they would set this up as the maypole. It was decorated with ribbons and a garland of flowers, and later in the day people would dance around it. One of the young girls of the village would be chosen as 'Queen of the May'. She would preside over the festivities from a special flower-covered throne in a leafy bower.

Flower garlands

What you need
Old newspapers, green crêpe paper, coloured tissue paper, adhesive, sticky tape.

What to do
Take sheets of newspaper and roll them up to make crumpled tubes. Form these into a circle, holding them together with sticky tape. Add more newspaper tubes until you have a good thick circle of paper. Cut long strips of green crêpe paper and let the children help you to wind these tightly all around the circle until the newspaper is completely covered. You or the children can then cut flower shapes from the tissue paper and they can stick them on to the green wreath. You can also add coloured ribbons if you wish and then display these garlands all around the classroom.

Wigan Floral Dance

What you need
A large green PE hoop, assorted paper flowers, sticky tape.

What to do
Morris dancers are particularly associated with May Day and although the dress may vary, most of them wear hats with ribbons, carry large handkerchiefs and have bells tied on to their legs. Their dances contain lots of stamping and kicking to make the bells ring loudly. This was supposed to wake the spirits of the ground after the winter, to drive away evil spirits and, hopefully, to ensure a good harvest.

Making the floral arch
Open the hoop at its join to make an arch which can be held by two children. Use sticky tape to attach the paper flowers all over the hoop, leaving about 20cm hand spaces at each end.

The dance
All the class can join in this dance and chant the rhyme. Two children are chosen to hold the arch and the rest form a long line each holding hands with the child in front and behind them. They all skip or dance round and through the arch chanting this rhyme:

May Day, May Day
Bright or grey day,
Hear the children sing and shout.
Dancing one behind the other,
If the flowers fall . . .
You're out!

At this last line, which is shouted, the arch holders let the arch fall in front of the child passing under it and that child then has to stand behind one of the arch holders, holding his or her waist. Those who are 'out' should go to alternate arch holders so that at the end the class is divided equally between the two. Finally, the arch is put down and the game ends with a tug-of-war.

Other dances
Formal country dances are often a little difficult for most in this age group, so start them off with simple versions using combinations of three movements.
- The circle — all the dancers join hands and skip round in a circle to the music.
- skipping on the spot — turn to the next dancer, join crossed hands facing each other and then skip round on the spot.
- The parade — stay holding crossed hands with a partner and turn to the front to walk and then skip round in a circle (clockwise or anti-clockwise), following the couple in front.

Use any traditional English or Scottish dance music which has a slow regular beat. Let the children carry on each movement longer than the normal four or eight beats and then stop the music to organise them into the next movement and carry on when they are ready. It takes great co-ordination to change to the next movement quickly, but practice makes perfect. The main thing is to help the children complete the movements, listen to the music and enjoy the group activity.

Kodomo-no-hi

This day (5 May) has traditionally been the boys' counterpart to Hinamatsuri, and was known as 'Boys' Day' (Tangonosekku), but it has now been designated as 'Children's Day'. Kites made in the shape of carp are flown from poles in people's gardens and there will usually be one kite for each son. The largest and most beautiful one being for the oldest boy. The carp is chosen because it is supposed to be strong and brave, and also be blessed with long life, qualities which are to be encouraged in the boys. The iris flower is also an important symbol for this time, its leaves being shaped like the blades of the swords once used by brave warriors. On this day, models of Samurai helmets and armour are presented and displayed. Health-giving foods are eaten: *kashiwamochi* (rice cakes filled with sweet bean paste and wrapped in oak leaves) or *chimaki* (rice cakes wrapped in cogon grass or bamboo leaves). This reinforces the overall idea of health and strength which is celebrated at the festival.

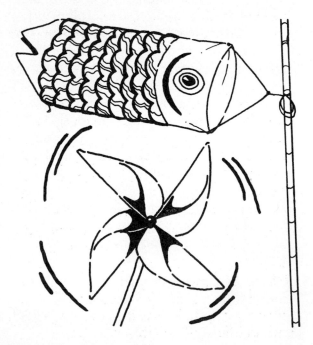

Carp streamers

What you need
Sheets of coloured activity paper or sugar paper, adhesive, scissors, paints or other colouring materials, fish scales cut from coloured foil, garden canes.

What to do
Help the children to fold the sheets of activity paper in half lengthways and stick them together along their longest edges. Guide them to cut out the tail sections and decorate the tubes to look like carp. Show them how to add some of the coloured foil scales in rows, starting at the tail. Tie the finished carp streamers to garden canes and let them blow in the wind.

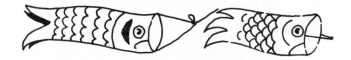

Paper windmill

What you need
15cm x 15cm paper squares, pencil, scissors, drawing pins, adhesive.

What to do
Mark the diagonals of each paper square and let the children try to cut along them from the points of the square stopping 2.5cm short of the centre.

Help them to bend over, but not press flat, each alternate point of their square to the centre and stick them in place. When the adhesive is dry, push a drawing pin through the centre of each windmill and fix it to the garden cane, supporting their carp streamer. Make sure there is enough space for the pinwheel to turn.

Foods for health and strength

What you need
Pictures of foodstuffs.

What to do
Talk about favourite foods and discuss whether they are good for us. Link the importance of good, nutritious food and exercise to help us to grow strong and healthy. Talk about the effects on our teeth and gums of eating too many sweets and crisps and drinking too many sugary drinks. Invite the school nurse or doctor in to explain the need for good food, rest and exercise. Look at the effects of no food on starving people in other countries. Many children are allergic to specific foods or food additives, which upset the working of their bodies and cause a variety of reactions from asthma to rashes. Do the children know of any allergies they have? (If so, check this out with their parents for future reference).

Do be sensitive, during discussions about the effects of foods, to the feelings of children with weight problems, whether over- or underweight. Talk about how people vary in size and shape and how we should be tolerant of differences in appearance as well as lifestyle.

Set up a display of pictures of foods which are good for us and those which, if we eat too many, are very bad for us. Give the children the opportunity to sort the different pictures of foods into 'good' or 'bad', 'healthy' or 'unhealthy', by asking them to place the pictures in the correct hoops.

Wesak

Wesak is a Buddhist festival which takes place in the month of Visakha, usually in May or June. At this time Theravadan Buddhists celebrate the birth, enlightenment and death of Buddha. All these events took place on the same day, but in different years. There are two main groups of Buddhists, Mahayana and Theravadan. It is the Theravadan Buddhists who celebrate all three events on the same day. Their temples and homes are decorated with lanterns and flowers, and offerings of flowers are placed in front of statues of Buddha. There are processions in the temples with burning incense sticks and candles and a sermon telling the teachings of Buddha. The monks of the temple are shown great hospitality and generosity and sometimes, as a symbol of the love and compassion of Buddha, captured birds and fish are set free.

Looking after animals

What you need
School pet.

What to do
You may have a school pet which some of the children in the group help to look after. They could tell the others the sorts of things they do to care for the pet. Any children who have pets at home could bring them in, if possible, and talk about the way they look after them. Parents should bring in the pets of any younger children to ensure safety and it is wise to consult the DFE and local education authority regulations regarding the care and handling of animals in school.

Collage of living things

What you need
Paper, crayons or felt-tipped pens, reference books about animals, display materials.

What to do
Remind the children that Buddha taught that we should be kind to all living creatures. Talk about living things, plants and flowers, animals and birds, and let the children draw pictures of their favourites. Encourage older children to look for books with suitable illustrations to help them make accurate drawings. They can also include a brief descriptive passage to explain why they like their particular choice. These can then be displayed, after discussion about suitable backgrounds, to show the animals and plants in their usual habitats.

Shavuot

This is an ancient Jewish harvest festival which takes place in May or June. When the Jewish people were travelling through the wilderness with Moses, they were given many laws, some of which related to the giving of the first fruits of the harvest as a thank offering. One of these harvest festivals is Shavuot (also known as Pentecost or the Feast of Weeks). Shavuot takes place seven weeks after Passover and is at the end of the barley harvest and the beginning of the wheat harvest.

This is also the time of year when Moses was given the Ten Commandments on Mount Sinai, the laws on which both the Jewish and Christian religions are based. For the Jews these laws are presented in the Torah, their holy book, so this festival gives thanks for food for the mind and the body.

Synagogues are decorated with fruit. Dairy products and honey are the traditional foods at this time to remind the people that there was little meat or fish in the wilderness as they travelled towards the 'land of milk and honey', which was Israel. (It is also said that Moses took so long to tell the people the new rules of their faith that the milk turned to cheese!)

Our rules

What you need
Card, colouring materials.

What to do
The Ten Commandments are the rules for life described in the Torah.

Talk with the children about the rules we have for living together, school rules and the laws of the land. Start off by discussing the home, perhaps with bedtimes. Who makes the rules in the children's homes and are there different rules for different family members? The older children in this age group will be starting to have opinions about fair play and will understand a little of the need for rules. However, it is still a fruitful exercise with the youngest to encourage discussion about their own lives. Relate the use of rules to the classroom situation and look around the room to see where rules are most obviously used, for example in different play areas. You may have a rule about the numbers of children allowed in one area at any one time, such as 'Only three children in the paint area'. Discuss such rules and the reasons why they are necessary. You and the children may find areas where a rule is needed for guidance, for example a quiet writing, reading or listening corner may need a 'Please be quiet here.' request in the form of a notice.

Pentecost

Pentecost was, and is, a Jewish feast taken over and given another meaning by the Christian Church. For Jews it is a harvest festival and is called the Feast of Weeks. The Christian festival celebrates the day on which the Holy Spirit came to Jesus' disciples and gave them power to continue the work that Jesus started. Pentecost is also known as 'Whit Sunday', this name comes from 'White Sunday', so called because people would dress in white to be baptised into the Christian Church. This was a favourite day to be baptised, even though it could be done at any time of the year. Whit Monday was a popular day for fairs and parish walks, but most of the activities associated with that day are now held on the Spring Bank Holiday instead.

Fire can change things

What you need
A selection of objects made of different materials (two examples of each), a large open space where you can build a bonfire, wood and other materials to build the bonfire.

What to do
One of the outward signs of the presence of the Holy Spirit with the disciples of Jesus was said to have been tongues of flame above their heads. The Holy Spirit gave the disciples the strength and courage to continue the work of Jesus, and also enabled them to communicate in many foreign languages. Talk to the children about fire as a symbol of strength and power.

Then build a bonfire, making sure that you site it well away from buildings or trees. Put the collection of objects in or on to the bonfire. Include a metal spoon, a plastic cup, a leather shoe, an old mug, and an old telephone directory and put some potatoes in a large biscuit tin. Keep the second set of objects in the classroom so that you can compare them with the set that has been in the fire. Make sure that the children stand well clear of the fire and then light it. (You can use the actual experience of watching the bonfire to stimulate creative writing.) Encourage the children to observe the swirling smoke, the dancing sparks and the leaping flames and to listen to the crackling wood. Watch the fire as it dies down and look at the glowing embers and the silver ashes. Leave the fire to die out completely, preferably overnight.

The next day return with the children to the bonfire and, after making sure that the fire is completely out and absolutely cold, sift through the ashes to try and find the remains of the objects you put in. Some objects will hardly have changed at all, there will only be parts of some objects remaining, and of others there will be no trace. The potatoes in the tin will have been cooked through and you can collect all the things together to take back to the classroom to compare with the other set of objects. Give the children magnifying glasses to look closely at the objects and ask them to talk about what they see. Remember to stress safety and the dangers associated with fire. Remind the children that this activity is a science experiment and not a game.

Streamers

What you need
Garden canes, strips of red, white and blue tissue paper, sticky tape.

What to do
When children used to take part in Whit Walks, the spectators would have brightly coloured streamers like these to wave.

Help the children to attach the strips of tissue paper with sticky tape to the end of the garden canes.

Fiery words

What you need
Large sheet of orange paper, smaller pieces of red and yellow paper, adhesive, black marker pen, twigs.

What to do
Cut out flame shapes from the red and yellow paper and stick these on to the large sheet of orange paper to look like the flames of a bonfire, sticking on the twigs underneath to be the wood. Alternatively, draw the flames and wood shapes on to the large sheet of paper using the marker pen.

Discuss 'fire' with the children, to draw from them descriptive words such as: hot, red, sparks, flames, bright, dangerous and so on. As you talk, write a word on to each of the flames so that you produce a visual record of the discussion.

World Environment Day

World Environment Day is a secular celebration held on 5 June. It is good for children to think about our world and, most important for the young children, their own immediate environment. We can start to raise their awareness by taking a walk around school, on the playground or playing field.

Looking for litter

What you need
Large plastic sacks, disposable rubber gloves.

What to do
Take a walk around the school and encourage the children to pick up litter as they go, avoiding broken glass as this would be too dangerous. If the children do this, they *must* wear strong, disposable rubber gloves. Collect all the litter together to see just how much there is and talk about where you found the most litter. Remind the children where the litter bins are located. Discuss what would happen if no one bothered about litter and talk about the need for lids on litter bins to stop the rubbish being blown about.

Suggest that the children draw a litter monster, with the parts of its body made up of the most commonly found pieces of litter. They could use this as a check list as they walk around and colour in or tick off the items of litter as they find them.

Older children may want to design anti-litter posters. Talk about current cartoon programmes with an environmental theme. Perhaps you could watch an episode of one of these to encourage discussion and to raise awareness of the problems of pollution. The children could invent their own cartoon environment team, or maybe design a machine that gobbles up litter and pollution and which can solve all Earth's problems. Younger children can use construction toys or Plasticine to make their machines, while older ones could try drawing their designs. They will have great fun describing how they work. The designs and models could be displayed to coincide with World Environment Day.

Talk about recycling. Try to find examples of recycled paper. Some schools organise collections of old newspapers and aluminium cans. Ask the children to look out for bottle banks at supermarkets. All these things will help the children to understand the need to be careful with the resources of our planet to help safeguard their future.

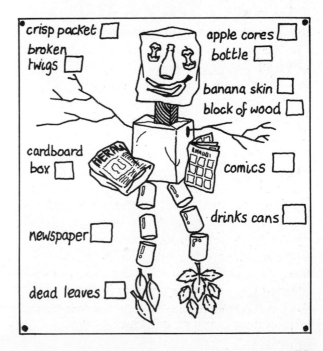

Father's Day

Father's Day is a secular celebration and is quite a recent innovation. It is the male equivalent of Mother's Day and is celebrated on the first Sunday after Trinity Sunday. On this day families often get together to say thank you to their fathers. They usually send cards and give gifts to show their appreciation for all the things their fathers have done for them during the year. The children may try to do extra jobs around the house or in the garden or perhaps they may help their dads, for example, to wash the car. The important thing to stress is that we should appreciate both our parents all through the year not just on their special days.

You may need to make the point that it is not the child's fault if he or she does not have a father at home, merely a fact of life and, as such, an acceptable lifestyle. Emphasise the importance and validity of other male carers, such as step-fathers and grandfathers, if necessary.

Father's Day card

What you need
Pieces of card 16cm x 24cm, coloured pens or pencils or paint, adhesive, gold foil, scissors, paper.

What to do
Fold the card as shown below.

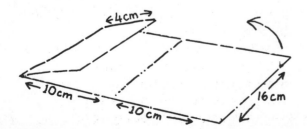

Let the children decorate the outsides of their cards to look like treasure chests by colouring or painting them brown and, when dry, sticking on corners cut from the gold foil. Cut out lock shapes for the overlapping parts and stick these in place. Inside the card, you (or the children if they are able) should write the words: 'Happy Father's Day from your little treasure.' Encourage the children to decorate all around the words with pictures of jewels and gold, or shapes cut from the coloured foil to represent them.

Father's Day notepad

What you need
Squares of card 20cm x 20cm, ready-mixed or powder paints, PVA adhesive, cardboard combs, small notepads or several sheets of plain white paper stapled together, pencil, strong thin cord, sticky tape.

What to do
Give each child a square of card to paint all over with a 1:1 mixture of paint and PVA adhesive. Then let the children use the cardboard combs to create patterns on the surface and leave them to dry. Take the small notepads or stapled sheets of paper and stick them in place. Tie the cord to the pencil and attach the end of the cord to the back of the square of card with sticky tape. A small piece of Blu-Tack on the back of the pencil will hold it in place, next to the notepad, until it is required for use. Older children will be able to do this for themselves, but younger ones will only be able to do the painting.

Tuan Yang Chieh

The Dragon Boat Festival, Tuan Yang Chieh, is a Chinese festival which usually occurs in June. It is a time when people remember how an important statesman and poet, rather than agree with what the then Emperor was doing, decided to throw himself from a cliff into a lake, where he drowned. The people liked him so much that they saved his body from being eaten by fish and demons by throwing lumps of rice into the water and making a great deal of noise to scare them away. In China, local villages and towns hold special boat races in boats decorated with dragon heads and the people often eat rice dumplings wrapped in leaves.

A dragon boat

What you need
Margarine tubs, Plasticine, sheets of paper, colouring materials, plastic straws, adhesive, sticky tape, paper clips, water trough.

What to do
Give each child a sheet of paper on which to draw and colour in a picture of a dragon. This is the sail. Challenge the children to devise a way of fixing the mast (a plastic straw) to their boat (a margarine tub). Let them choose from the adhesive materials suggested and allow them to experiment.

You can then hold your own boat races around the water trough. You could also experiment with different shaped sails to see if one shape is better than the others.

Floating and sinking

What you need
A large variety of different objects of all shapes and sizes, water trough, a table.

What to do
Place the items near the water trough and ask the children to test to see which items float and which sink. Ask them to watch out for those objects which do not float on top of the water, but half submerged. Look at the way different objects float; compare a wet sponge with a dry sponge. Talk about the way things sink; some go straight down to the bottom, others sink very slowly. Some things float or sink depending upon how they are placed into the water. Younger children can simply sort and classify the objects on a nearby table, but older children can perhaps offer reasons why the things float or sink.

Sing some songs associated with boats to follow up this activity; for example, 'Messing about on the river', 'Row, row, row your boat', 'We are sailing' or 'Michael, row your boat ashore'.

61

St Swithun's Day

It is said that if it rains on St Swithun's Day, 15 July, then it is likely to be wet for the next 40 days. St Swithun was the Bishop of Winchester, from AD 852 but he did not like all the trappings of being a bishop, so he asked that when he died he should be buried outside the cathedral, so that everyone who came to worship would walk on his grave. After he died his wish was granted, but soon afterwards his body was moved inside the cathedral by the monks and it is supposed to have rained for 40 days. People said that this happened because St Swithun did not like being moved against his wishes.

Look at puddles

What you need
Chalk (or a saucer of water, black waterproof felt-tipped pen).

What to do
Go outside on a bright day after a wet period and look for a large puddle. Mark the size of the puddle by drawing a chalk line all the way around the edge. Go out again after a couple of hours and see if the puddle has become smaller. If it has, draw another line around the new limit of the water. Ask the children where the water has gone.

You can do a similar experiment in the classroom by placing a saucer of water on a sunny window ledge or on top of the radiator and marking the levels with a black waterproof felt-tipped pen.

Weather poems

What you need
Examples of weather-lore poetry.

What to do
This poem is often said around St Swithun's Day:

St Swithun's Day, if thou dost rain,
For 40 days it will remain.
St Swithun's Day, if thou be fair,
For 40 days 'twill rain no more.

There are many little rhymes which tell us about the weather, such as:

When cows are standing in the fields,
a dry day you can claim.
But when you see them lying down,
'tis sure a sign of rain.

Others are:

Red sky at night, shepherd's delight.
Red sky in the morning, sailor's warning.

Or:

Rain by seven, fine by eleven.

Encourage the children to test any of these or other examples of weather lore.

Talk about the use of plants to help us to try and guess the weather. Look at pine cones. They are supposed to close up if rain is expected. Explain to the children that these things are not as reliable as the weather forecast on television. Look at a barometer too to see how well it can predict the weather.

Obon

This is a Japanese Mahayana Buddhist festival, held in some places in August and in others in July. It is a happy family festival when the spirits of the ancestors are welcomed home on an annual visit. They are thought of in a happy way rather than being sad that they are dead, and their annual visit is celebrated with lanterns, bonfires on the hillsides and special offerings of food delicacies, as well as herbs and flowers on the family altars. At the end of the festival, the people participate in a traditional circular folk dance. In the city of Hiroshima, the spirits of those newly departed are guided on their way to spirit homes by floating tiny candles in paper boats, which are set sailing on the river at night.

Family talk

What you need
A quiet place to talk.

What to do
In common with many religions, Buddhists believe that those who die live again in a spirit world and this festival celebrates a belief in communication with that world.

Depending on the present family circumstances of individual children and your assessment of their reaction, introduce the topic of the death of a loved one. Sometimes if an adult relates an experience of their own about the death of an elderly relative or a pet, the children may volunteer comments or stories of their own experience. The death of a pet can often prepare children to handle the, sometimes, more traumatic loss of a human family member.

Floating candles

What you need
Mouldable wax, wicks, large glass bowl of water.

What to do
Mouldable wax has a very low melting point enabling it to be moulded easily, softened by the warmth of the children's hands. It comes in bright colours and one pack is sufficient for 15 floating candles.

Mouldable wax is brittle when cold and easily broken into individual pieces, which, after a few minutes handling, become very malleable. To make a candle, roll a piece of softened wax into a thick sausage shape and lay a small piece of wick at one end with a little hanging over each edge. Next roll the wax up with the wick sticking up when the wax coil is laid on its side. Now float the candle in a large bowl of water. You may need to experiment with the stability of the candles as an uneven distribution of weight may tip them into the water. Solutions include pressing the bottom of the candle into an eggcup to give a rounded shape or, alternatively, placing the candle on a small, stable container.

Light the candles for a shimmering effect on the water's surface. Do observe strict safety precautions at all times with lighted candles. (Mouldable wax is available from Specialist Crafts Limited, PO Box 247, Leicester LE1 9QS.)

Raksha bandhan

This is a Hindu festival, which many Sikhs also celebrate. It takes place in July or August and is a day when sisters honour their brothers and in return brothers promise to protect their sisters. *Raksha* means 'to protect' and *bandhan* means 'to tie'. On this day sisters tie a band of red and gold thread, called a *rakhi*, around their brothers' wrists, and mark their brothers foreheads with red powder, with a prayer that they may protect the men from all evils. The brothers, in turn, promise to protect their sisters.

The custom is said to be derived from an ancient Hindu story about Indra, king of the lesser gods. Indra's wife was given such a thread by the god Vishnu to tie on her husband's right wrist and so protect him in his battle with the strong demon king, Bali. Indra was victorious because of this amulet and regained his kingdom.

Families sometimes combine this festival with Coconut Day (Nariyal Purnima). Coconuts are considered to be sacred and this festival marks the end of the rainy season, when fishermen offer coconuts to Varuna, the sea god.

Make a rakhi

What you need
Strips of paper (3cm wide and long enough to fit around a child's wrist), lengths of red and yellow wool, clear self-adhesive plastic film, hole punch, red and yellow pencils or felt-tipped pens or crayons.

What to do
Trim each strip of paper to fit the wrist of a child, but allowing for the band to be tied. Then let the children decorate the paper strips with red and yellow patterns of their choice. Cover the strips with the self-adhesive plastic film to give them strength. Younger children will obviously need help with this, but is just a matter of folding the plastic film over so that it can be trimmed of any excess later. Punch a hole at each end of the strips and thread through some red and yellow wool with which to tie the bands on.

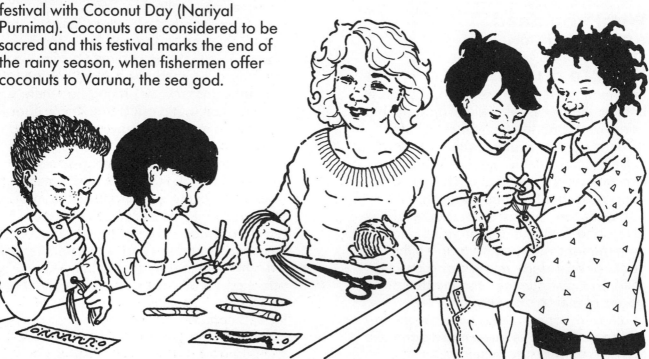

Coconut pyramids

What you need
Bowl, grater, baking tray, wooden spoon, eggcup.
Ingredients
(For about 24 pyramids.)
2 eggs
200g (6½oz) dried coconut
100g (3oz) sugar
Rind and juice of half a lemon

What to do
Beat the sugar and the eggs together and then add the coconut, grated lemon rind and lemon juice and mix thoroughly. Shape the mixture into pyramids by pressing a small quantity into a moistened eggcup and arrange them on a baking tray. Bake at 375°F/190°C or Gas Mark 5 for 15–20 minutes until lightly browned.

 These cakes are an ideal way to celebrate Coconut Day.

My family

What you need
Art materials.

What to do
With all the children or in small groups, talk about 'My family'. Let the children say how many people are in their families, with particular reference to brothers and sisters. They can discuss the sorts of things they like to do together, and the places they go to as a family. Let them paint family portraits and display these as your portrait gallery. If the children are able, they can write the names of the members of their families underneath their pictures. Older children can make sets of the names of children in the class who have brothers or sisters, with an intersection to show those children who have both. They will have to think about where the children who have no brothers or sisters should go. You could also collect information to make a picture graph to show family size. This will also give an indication of those children who have brothers and sisters.

Janamashtami

This Hindu festival commemorates Krishna's birth and falls between July and September. The word 'janamashtami' means 'eighth day of birth'. Krishna is a symbol of love, who fights against evil and loves life, so this is a time of great happiness and enjoyment.

Krishna is said to have been born at midnight, so many Hindus fast and stay up until the midnight celebrations to greet the baby Krishna. They go to the temple to see children acting out stories of Krishna, or to hear stories about him, and just before midnight a statue of the infant Krishna is washed with a mixture of ghee, yoghurt, milk, sugar and honey. This mixture is then collected and everyone gets to share it. A statue or picture of the infant Krishna is placed in a decorated cradle or on a decorated swing, and everyone files past to rock the cradle or push the swing. There is a ceremony performed at midnight with lamps and ringing bells. Sweets are given out and everyone joins in a special feast.

One of the stories often told about the festival's origin, tells of how the demon king, Kamsa, decided to kill all the children born to his sister, Devaki, because he had been told that one of them would kill him. Devaki and her husband were imprisoned and Kamsa killed each child as it was born. Just before the birth of her eighth child, Krishna, Devaki persuaded her sister to exchange babies. When Kamsa came to kill Krishna, his father escaped with him and the special baby girl flew up into the air telling Kamsa that Krishna was safe and would one day return to kill him.

Krishna's cradle

What you need
Selection of cardboard boxes, small doll to represent Krishna, tissue paper, crêpe paper, scraps of material, glitter, sequins, tinsel, coloured foil, adhesive, scissors, paint, sticky tape.

What to do
Let the children choose a suitably sized box for the doll to fit in. This can be a group or individual activity. They can then paint the box and decorate it with tissue paper flowers, crêpe paper frills, sequins, glitter, tinsel or shiny foil.

Older children could try to construct a decorated swing. Give them the opportunity to experiment using junk materials to find out a way of constructing the swing for themselves.

September – December

Chapter three

The festivals during the months from September to December are covered in this third section. These months coincide with the season of autumn and the beginning of winter in the Northern hemisphere. There are many harvest festivals and festivals of thanksgiving included in this section, since, traditionally, this is the time when the crops were gathered. There are festivals of light, such as Diwali, and the Bonfire Night celebrations of 5 November, and the section culminates with the celebration of Christmas. Many of the festivals include light and fire and would be very useful for lighting up the darkening days.

Ganesha Chaturthi

This festival celebrates the birthday of Ganesha Chaturthi, the elephant-headed god of wisdom and prosperity. He is the remover of obstacles and Hindus pray to him before they start anything new which is important to them, such as taking examinations, moving house or getting married. Ganesh's birthday is celebrated on the fourth day of the Hindu month of Bhadrapada, which usually falls in September.

Ganesh mask

What you need
Paper plates, garden canes, grey paint, card or thick paper, adhesive, silver foil, glitter, sequins.

What to do
For each mask, cut two elephant's ears from card and also a long strip, 6cm wide, for the trunk. Let the children assemble their elephants' heads by sticking the ears to the backs of the paper plate and painting the whole grey. They should also paint the paper strips. When the strips are dry, show the children how to fold them into concertina shapes and stick one to the front of each paper plate as the trunk. They should add eyes and tusks cut from silver foil. Cut head-dress shape from the card and tell the children to paint them in a bright colour and then decorate them with the sequins and glitter and attach them to the elephants' heads. Attach a garden cane to the back of each elephant mask so that the children can hold it in front of their faces.

Ethiopian New Year

New year is celebrated by Rastafarians worldwide on 11 September. They are guided by the culture and traditions of Ethiopia. Rastafari is a way of life and not, strictly speaking, a religion, but it shares many beliefs with the Jewish and Christian faiths. For example, Christmas is celebrated, not as Jesus' birthday but as an acknowledgement of his life and work. The Ethiopian calendar is used by Rastafarians and has 13 months, the years being named in a four year cycle after the apostles, Matthew, Mark, Luke and John. New Year is celebrated by all the generations in the family with singing, dancing, drumming and prayer. There is plenty of good food as well.

Rastafari

What you need
Card, black paper, brown parcel paper, small objects with which to print, red, yellow and green paint (the colours of the Ethiopian flag), shallow paint containers.

What to do
Rastafarians like to wear clothes in the African tradition, preferring simple styles and the colours of the Ethiopian flag; red, golden yellow and green. African clothes are worn on special festivals and white on most holy days.

Draw a figure about 25cm high on to card and then cut this out. Now help the children who are able, to use this as a template to draw a figure on to black paper which can also be cut out, preferably by the child. This is the Rastafarian person.

To make a simple robe, the child needs to cut out a long T-shirt shape in brown parcel paper, big enough to fit the figure. Put a little of each colour of paint in the shallow containers and, using any small scrap objects or potatoes cut into different two-dimensional shapes, let the children print simple all-over designs with the three colours. These shapes can then be lightly stuck to the figures.

Rastafarians cover their hair, women and girls wear an Ethiopian-style scarf and/or both sexes wear the knitted hat called a 'tam'. Make such a hat for the figure by cutting out a curved oval and finger-painting it, using stripes of the three colours. Stick the tam on to the head of the figure with a little adhesive, as before.

Display the figures around the room holding hands as a frieze, or around the edge of a poster about Rastafarians.

Mango ice-cream

What you need
Bowls, metal spoon, wooden spoon, lidded plastic box, whisk.

Ingredients
4 eggs, separated
120g (4oz) caster sugar
300ml (½pint) double cream
2 mangoes or 2 medium cans mango pulp
1 tsp lemon juice

What to do
Prepare the freezer by turning it up to maximum or 'fast freeze'. Cut the mangoes in half and scoop out the flesh and then pulp it in a bowl. Alternatively, use tinned mangoes. The egg whites should be whisked until stiff, adding the sugar just before the final whisking. In a separate bowl, whisk the cream until thick and then add the egg yolks one at a time, whisking a little after each. Next, the cream mixture should be folded gently into the egg white with a metal spoon, taking care not to deflate the whites.

Finally, add the mangoes and the lemon juice in the same gentle way and pour the mixture into a plastic box with a lid. This mixture needs to be frozen for 1½ hours and then removed and whisked thoroughly. Return the ice-cream to the box and freeze it until it is solid.

A Rastafarian lunch
Rastafarian people are strict about their diet and eat no meats, preservatives, additives, salt or alcohol and prefer organically-grown food. They eat many foods in the Caribbean tradition.

If you work in a school or nursery that provides lunch, let the children help to prepare a Rastafarian meal. Use any vegetarian dishes, fresh salads and baked potatoes and finish with the ice-cream. Alternatively, make peanut or banana bread.

Rastafarians like African foods such as plantains, yams, cassava root and maize. There are now many recipe books available which cater for international tastes such as Caribbean.

Drums and reggae

What you need

Paint (red, green, yellow), PVA adhesive, coffee or baby-milk tins with plastic lids, Reggae music recordings, tape recorder.

What to do

Music is an important part of the Rastafarian lifestyle at weekly meetings and special occasions. Drumming is part of the African heritage and accompanies hymns, songs and dancing. When Rastafarians come together to drum and chant it is called 'nyahbinghi' and Reggae music is based on this tradition. Listen to some Reggae music and let the children move freely to the beat. Simply listening carefully to something which may be different from their own experience will be fun and the strong beat of this music is exciting and compels movement. If possible, invite an African dance troupe into school for the children to watch.

Make a drum

Mix two parts PVA adhesive to one part paint, to make plastic paint which adheres to metal and plastic and use this to decorate the tins for the base of the drums. The children can use any designs they like with the three Rastafarian colours. Let these dry thoroughly before putting on the lids to complete the drums. The children can then accompany the Reggae music freely by tapping on the lids of the tins and you can also show them simple rhythms: 2/4 (two beats in a bar, that is 1,2, 1,2, . . .) and 4/4 (four beats in a bar, that is 1,2,3,4, 1,2,3,4 . . .).

Grandparent's Day

Grandparent's Day, like Father's Day, is quite a recent introduction in this country. It is a day on which to think about all the kindness shown by our grandmother and grandfather. On this day, cards and gifts are sent to say thank you, and grandparents are visited or taken out for a special treat or meal. In many other countries, grandparents are treated with great respect. In Japan 15 September is a public holiday – 'Keiro no hi' or 'Respect for the Aged Day'. As with the other special days in honour of members of our family, you should try to encourage the children to remember them all through the year and not only on this one day.

Grandparents' Day card

What you need

Card, coloured pencils, felt-tipped pens or paints, individual tea bag on a string, scissors, sticky tape.

What to do

Take a piece of card and fold it in half. Draw the shape of a large teapot or cup and saucer on one half and cut it out of the folded card, taking care not to cut along the fold. Older children may be able to do this themselves if they are provided with cardboard templates around which to draw. Let the children decorate their cards and write their greetings inside. Use the kind of individual tea bags which have a string attached and attach this to the inside of the card with sticky tape.

The way we were

What you need
A 'user-friendly' grandparent.

What to do
Invite one or two of the children's grandparents into school to talk about what school was like when they were young. They may have photographs, or books and toys which you can compare with modern toys. Make a display of the toys, and try to link it with a visit to a museum or heritage centre for some of the older children to experience a little of what life was like in the past; for example, Beamish: North of England Open Air Museum in County Durham, Wigan Pier in Lancashire or Ironbridge Gorge Museum in Shropshire are all such places where the children can gain first-hand experience. If the grandparents can accompany the children on these trips, they will help the children to identify more easily with the things they see.

Rosh Hashanah

Rosh Hashanah is the Jewish New Year and it is celebrated on two days in September or early October. It is the beginning of the most important time in the Jewish religious year, the ten day period leading up to the 'Day of Atonement', Yom Kippur. As it is New Year, there are many customs which involve renewal and starting again. People will often buy a new outfit and make New Year resolutions to change some aspect of their life. They will exchange the greeting 'Shanah tova' which means 'Good year'. At home they may dip an apple in honey and eat it for a sweet year and some families make a special bread (hallot). Rosh Hashana is welcomed with the blowing of the shofar or ram's horn, in remembrance of Abraham sacrificing a ram instead of his son. It calls the Jewish people to remember God and their fellow men, to remember their belief that God created the world and is also judge of what we do in our everyday lives, so it is a good time for thinking of ways to make our lives better.

Make a megaphone

What you need
Activity paper, adhesive, large open space.

What to do
The *shofar* is used to call people to worship. Its shape is important as the sound must start at the narrow end and come from the wide end, this is the principle used in a megaphone which can help to amplify sounds. Although the *shofar* is supposed to be curved and not straight (to remind people of the Jews' willingness to submit to God), we can explore how sounds can be amplified by making a simple megaphone.

Take the children outside into the playground and let them try shouting to one another while some distance apart. Talk about how the direction of the sound is important in order to help people to hear. Let the children try using cupped hands to see if this helps.

Back inside, make a cone shape from activity paper and let the children experiment to see if this makes any difference to the sound that is made. Test the megaphone outside to see if the distance over which a call can be heard is improved by its use.

Yom Kippur

Nine days after Rosh Hashanah is Yom Kippur, the Day of Atonement. This is the holiest day of the Jewish year and is marked by 24 hours of fasting, prayer, and asking God to forgive sins. The night before, all the family gathers together for a special meal. Festive candles called 'Yahrzeit candles' are lit, and members of the family ask each other for forgiveness for anything they have done wrong. After the meal everyone goes to the synagogue to pray.

Next day, people who can fast for the whole day. Invalids, old people and young children may be excused from fasting. From early morning until sunset, a service is held and at sunset the *shofar* is blown again to mark the end of the fast.

Helping each other

What you need
No special requirements.

What to do
Explain to the children that this is the time of year when members of Jewish families say sorry to each other for any unkind thing they may have done. Discuss any occasions when the children may have felt sad because of what someone else has done to them. Talk about what makes them happy. Encourage them to try to do things for other people to make them happy as well. They can illustrate this with pictures of something that makes them happy, or what they think they could do to help others. Older children could list their ideas to go with their pictures.

Durga Puja/ Dusserah/ Ram Lila

This festival is celebrated over ten days in September or October. Durga Puja, sometimes called Navaratri, is the first nine nights and Dusserah is the tenth. It is a joint celebration of Durga and Rama.

The festival commemorates the victory of Durga over the buffalo demon, Mahishasura, and the victory of Rama over the demon king, Ravana. Durga was the female champion of all the gods, whom they sent to kill Mahishasura. She was given special weapons to help her: Shiva's trident, Vishnu's disc, Yama's spear, Agni's dart, a magical bow from Vayu, a quiver full of arrows from Surya, a sword and a shield from Kala, a club from Kubera, and Indra's thunderbolt. She also had some armour from Vishnu and rode on a ferocious lion. After a fierce struggle, she defeated the demon.

The Ram Lila plays are based on the stories from the Ramayana. The festival reaches its climax when arrows are fired into a nine metre tall figure of Ravana, the ten-headed demon king, to celebrate the victory of Rama over Ravana.

Act the story of Durga

What you need
A children's version of the story of Durga and Mahishasura, cloaks for simple costumes, props for each of the items given to Durga by the gods: the trident, the disc, a spear, a dart, a bow and arrows, a sword, a shield, a club and a thunderbolt.

What to do
Choose one child for each of the parts, including Durga and all the gods and goddesses who gave the special weapons. You will also need someone to play the part of Mahishasura. Read the story and let the children improvise the actions as you go along. Older children might like to add a little dialogue as they give the weapons to Durga. The story can culminate in the fierce battle between Durga and Mahishasura with Durga triumphant.

Ten-headed Ravana

What you need
Very large sheet of paper, paint, paper plates, raffia, coloured foil, tissue paper, glitter, sequins.

What to do
It is not necessary to make the figure of Ravana nine metres tall, as large as possible will suffice. Let some of the children be involved in painting and decorating the large body shape while others are making ten faces with the paper plates. Encourage the children to make the faces as horrible as they can, and they need not look the same. They could use the raffia for hair and make each face three-dimensional by sticking on a triangular paper nose and brightly coloured head-dress, decorated with coloured foil and glitter. When it is completed, mount the figure on the wall and surround him with golden arrows, as if they are being fired straight at him.

Harvest Home

Harvest Home is celebrated in the Christian church some time during October. This was the time of year when, in temperate climates such as Britain, before modern mechanised agricultural methods, the cereal harvest was made. However, today the cereal crops are harvested and even re-sown in August, but the tradition remains.

In Britain, from the earliest cereal harvest, it has been the custom to try to ensure a continuing harvest for the following season by making offerings to the goddess of the Earth and, as a curious mixture of Pagan and Christian, the last stoop of corn was cut and ceremonially carried to the church where it was kept for the whole of the following season. As time went on, this last cut was woven into a structure known as a 'corn dolly'. Originally the corn dolly was woman-shaped to represent the Earth goddess, but later each county developed its own, now traditional, design. These decorations were hung in both church and home for good luck.

On the last night of the harvest a huge harvest supper was prepared and the workers celebrated the bringing home of the harvest for the year's staple food supply. This custom began in medieval times and is still celebrated in many churches today. Nowadays churches and schools have harvest services and make displays of many types of foods, which may not be from Britain, but are distributed to the needy of a community as a symbolic share of the good fortune of the harvest. Prayers and songs of thanksgiving are offered too and often the church holds a Harvest supper and dance too. The main harvest in Christian countries round the world comes at different times of the year, but is celebrated in church with thanksgivings.

Visit a farm

What you need
Access to an arable or mixed farm, toy farm or farm play mat, toy farm animals and machinery.

What to do
Arrange to visit an arable farm or a mixed farm, where there is some crop production as well as animals. The summer term is best as the main cereal crops are then being harvested or are still standing in the fields so that the children can see them. Encourage the children to use all their senses; listening to the rustle of the wind through the crop, smelling the warm, musty scents, feeling the rough stalks and watching the wave-like ripples of the crop in the breeze.

Let them get as close as is safe to the machinery used, as its very size is impressive, even for an adult. This usually stimulates much discussion about size and power and the children's feelings too.

Schools television programmes often have features about harvest at this time of year and, if not, these programmes are sometimes available on video, so that you can show the children details of harvesting and transport and the use to which the crops are put.

As an extension activity, provide a toy farm with animals and vehicles for the children. You can talk together about what materials you could use for different fields and you could provide some cereal grains for the children to play with, perhaps loading the toy farm vehicles and storing the grains in containers like grain silos.

Making bread

What you need
Baking trays, bowl.
Ingredients
1¾kg (3½lb) white flour
3½tsp salt
30g (1oz) yeast
1tsp sugar
400ml (1¾pints) warm water

What to do
Grease the baking trays and put them to warm. Cream the yeast with the sugar and add to the warm water. Mix the salt and flour together and then make a well in the centre of the flour and pour the liquid into it. Sprinkle a little of the flour into the liquid to form a pool of batter and leave this to stand in a warm place for 20 minutes. Next mix in the rest of the flour to form an elastic dough, using more water if necessary. Knead the dough until it leaves the sides of the bowl clean. Put this bowl of dough in a warm place to rise, until the dough has doubled its size.

Turn the dough out on to a floured board and knead again, not too heavily, until there are only small holes in it. Now divide the dough with a knife into small portions, one for each child and show them how to form their dough into a round bun. These can be spaced out on the prepared trays and left to prove until they have doubled in size. Bake the buns in a hot oven (220°C/425°F or Gas Mark 7) for about 30 minutes or until they sound hollow when tapped and are light brown in colour.

To identify an individual's bun, spread cooking foil on the baking trays and carefully write the children's initials on this with a pencil next to each bun.

Breakfast time

What you need
An assortment of breakfast cereals, bowls, disposable spoons.

What to do
Ask the children each to bring in a small sample of their favourite breakfast cereal from home, as well as providing your own selection, including, if possible, a warm cereal such as porridge. Let the children sample as many of the cereals as they want to, encouraging them to compare the similarities and differences.

Using the cereal packets as labels for the sets, make a simple graph to show which children prefer which cereal. Make sets using circles of coloured paper. Stick the cereal packets to the circles with the names of the children who prefer each cereal on separate pieces of paper stuck underneath. Add the number of children too.

Sukkot

This is a Jewish harvest celebration held in September or October which commemorates the journey of the Jewish people through the wilderness after their exile in Egypt. They made 'sukkah' (huts or temporary dwellings) on their journey in which to take meals and to shelter. Today a Jewish family might make a decorative sukkah at harvest time.

Sukkah

What you need
A clothes-horse or play house frame, paper leaves and flower garlands, small tree branches, an old green sheet or bedspread, toy tea set, plastic fruit and vegetables.

What to do
Spread the sheet over the clothes-horse frame and decorate it with the paper flower garlands and leaves. Paper leaves can be stuck to the branches and these can be leaned against or put on top of the frame. The children can help make the sukkah each time it is played with or it can be left up in situ.

It can now be used as a home corner, in that the children can engage in family role-play; having a meal together, tidying up, sleeping and so on, as the Jews did long ago.

United Nations Day

The chief aim of the United Nations Organisation is to foster international peace through friendship and co-operation. The organisation was established on 24 October 1945, after the Second World War, and holds a commemorative day each year.

Dove of peace

What you need
White card, scissors, white crêpe paper, white paper.

What to do
The white dove is an international symbol of peace.

Show the children how to cut out the body shape of a bird, using a template if necessary, and cut a slit for them about 2½cm long in the middle of the body at the point where the wings should be. Give them each a piece of white paper (of a size that balances the body size) and tell them to concertina the paper along its length. To make the wings, they should keep the paper folded and feed it through the slit in the body, so that it is evenly balanced on each side, and then open out the wings gently for the in-flight position. Fix a narrow strip of white crêpe paper to the top of each bird so that it hangs in a well-balanced position and display several together, hanging from a PE hoop covered with white crêpe paper.

TV discussion

What you need
Short video extract from television news programme showing UN vehicles in a war zone, posters showing children of the world.

What to do
The UN tries to find peaceful solutions to international problems by discussion, as well as giving practical help. Video material is not absolutely necessary for this activity, but is useful to open-up discussion on how the UN tries to restore the peace and helps the needy with food and medicine. The content of any news coverage used should be ethically suitable for the age group. Many small children today are only too familiar with the more brutal television coverage of war and disaster. Material that you may consider suitable for children in this age group might be coverage of shellings and the dead and wounded in a war or street violence. Focusing attention on a short extract, to stimulate discussion, is an attempt to confront the issues in a simple, but positive way, by talking about what the children actually see and then thinking about their own lives and behaviour.

Encourage the children to talk about what they know of war already from television, parents and other sources. Many will only see the 'excitement' of soldiers running and the large machines they have. For the children this might seem like play. It is very difficult for children of this age to think in the abstract about how others might feel, but ask them to think how they feel if they are walking home and they are tired and hungry and cold or talk about feelings when they are angry, if there is a dispute in the playground or if they get hurt when someone else is causing trouble. Try to introduce them to the idea that people caught up in wars feel all these things, just like they do.

There are many situations in the daily lives of young children which mirror, for them, the horrors of war and when we, as adults, offer or impose different strategies for peaceful solutions. For example, any school bully or gang can feel like a hostile force and make the victim's life awful. In this discussion, perhaps the first of many which may arise spontaneously, talk about these situations and ask the children what they think are the kind and peaceful solutions to focus attention on the more positive values.

A prayer circle

What you need
National costumes, dolls in national dress, posters of children of the world.

What to do
Ask children with national costumes to wear them for the day and those with dolls dressed in national costumes to bring them in for a display. Try to get posters of children from different ethnic origins and let individual children, who have no doll or costume, hold them, so that all the children represent different parts of the world. Some children could hold paper doves of peace (see previous activity) or these could be included in a small display of posters and doves in the centre of the circle. The children could paint or draw pictures of different peoples living peacefully together or simply their own families and these could be shown or displayed too.

This simple event can be for any size group. Start off with everyone sitting in a circle, holding hands, to represent hands around the world, and sing a familiar song which has a peace or a family theme; for example, 'At half-past three we go home to tea' in *Someone's Singing, Lord* (1977, A&C Black). The family theme is most relevant for this age group. Now the leader can ask everyone to join in with a prayer for peace.

The children can repeat it in short sections. For example:

We ask our God for peace in the world and no more wars.
We ask that everyone might have food, a home and the happiness of family life.
We are the children of the world and we need love and peace in our lives.

Diwali

This Hindu New Year festival falls in October or November and is a time of new beginnings. It is also a festival of lights, when people remember the story of how Rama triumphed and freed his wife, Sita, from the demon king, Ravana; good winning over evil, light over darkness. In annual celebration, lamps and other lights are ceremoniously lit. Cities are illuminated with coloured electric lights and there are fireworks in the streets. In homes, small clay lamps called 'divas' are the traditional decoration, but in Western countries fairy lights and candles are also used. The lamps celebrate Rama and Sita's return and welcome Lakshmi, the traditional giver of prosperity, into the home at Diwali.

As with many faiths at the time of New Year, homes are cleaned and new clothes prepared for the festival.

The festival lasts for five days during which time presents are given, parties held and visits made to relations. As a time of new beginnings, shopkeepers open new books, craftsmen dedicate tools and all quarrels are settled.

Sikh people also keep this festival as this was the time when their sixth Guru, Hargobind, was released from prison by the Mogul Emperor. The Sikh people welcomed him home with candles and today the Golden Temple at Amristar is illuminated during the festival in his honour.

Diwali card

What you need
Red and white card, PVA adhesive, gold spray paint, gold and silver foil paper.

What to do
Fold rectangular pieces of red card in half. Cut semi-circles from white card and let the children dribble the adhesive across them in wavy lines or blobs to give a raised pattern when dry. This shape represents a clay *diva*. When the adhesive has hardened, spray it all over with gold paint. This should be carried out by an adult working in a well-ventilated area. Stick the *divas* on to the fronts of the red card and add two tongues of foil flame to each, a gold one inside a silver one. To complete the card, add a greeting inside, such as, 'Happy Diwali'.

Mehndi patterns

What you need
Different shades of brown art paper, shades of blue paint, small objects with which to print.

What to do
Mehndi patterns on hands and feet are a traditional decoration during festival times. They are drawn on to the skin with a small blunt stick using henna dye and last several weeks.

Ask the children each to draw round one of their hands and cut out the shape and then repeat this for the other hand. For those who can't yet manage all of this, help them to do as much as possible. Look at the different shades of brown paper and talk about skin colour variation within the class.

Using the blue paint and a variety of small scrap objects, let the children print overall designs on to the hand shapes. The youngest in the age group will find the concept of pattern difficult, but more-experienced children will be able to form simple repeating patterns on their hand shapes.

Rangoli patterns

What you need
White cartridge paper, wax crayons, white candle, thin black paint wash.

What to do
Rangoli patterns are drawn at the entrances to Hindu homes during Diwali to welcome the goddess Lakshmi. Traditionally, the patterns are drawn on the floor with chalk and filled in with coloured powders. They usually have two axes of symmetry.

As an alternative to the traditional powder patterns, cut the paper into 20cm squares and make a wax and wash (or wax resist) pattern on the paper. Ask the children to divide the squares with two axes of symmetry, using the wax crayons heavily. Let them add other decoration such as geometric shapes, keeping the symmetry. For very young children, make one of their lines extra thick and ask them to make the same shapes on either side of the central line. An adult should use the wax candle to trace over the children's colours to add extra protective wax. Finally, let the children wash over the patterns with the thin black paint to leave the wax pattern showing through.

Display these patterns as a border around the classroom door, during Diwali.

Bonfire Night

Bonfire Night is a British autumn celebration held on 5 November each year. It is sometimes called 'Guy Fawkes Night' because it has its origins in a historical event involving a man called Guy Fawkes. On this day in 1605, a group of men tried to blow up the Houses of Parliament and the unpopular king, James I. He was hated by many people because of his intolerance and cruelty towards people with different religious views. The leader of the plot was Robert Catesby, but Guy Fawkes was the one chosen to light the fuse to the gunpowder in the cellars of the Houses of Parliament. However, he was caught and put to death with several of the other conspirators.

Today, the Houses of Parliament are ceremoniously searched by the Yeomen of the Guard before a new Parliamentary session and on 5 November people light bonfires at night and sometimes burn a 'Guy' made of stuffed rags to remember the conspirators' bid for tolerance and to celebrate the fact that innocent people near the king were not killed. There are parties with fireworks, and toffee apples, treacle toffee and Parkin cake to eat and this autumn fire festival now seems to set the seal for the approach of wintertime.

Sparkling fireworks

What you need
Kitchen roll tubes, gummed paper shapes, paper art straws, assorted colours of glitter, PVA adhesive, large star sequins.

What to do
Cut the kitchen roll tubes to a variety of lengths for different-sized fireworks. Let the children explore the different tubes and the art straws and help them to recognise the tubes and straws as a set of cylinders. The children can then decorate the outsides of the tubes with the gummed shapes. Take this opportunity to discuss the shapes and colours.

Brush the art straws all over with adhesive and then tell the children to roll them in the glitter, which can be spread in shallow trays of different colours to prevent waste. Push some scrunched up paper into each of the decorated tubes and then show the children how to dip the ends of the straws in the adhesive and fit them between the edge of the paper and the side of the tube. Let the children use as many straws as will give the effect of coloured fire shooting from the tubes. They can also add sequin stars to the ends of the straws for extra glitter.

Take this opportunity to discuss safety and the Firework Code as you work.

Bonfire picture

What you need
Large sheets of dark blue paper (about 1.5m x 2m), red, orange, yellow and brown paint, large sponges, large paint brushes, black paper, scissors, red crêpe paper, yellow activity paper.

What to do
Position the dark blue paper on the wall at floor level so that the children can do all the paint work themselves without having to stand on anything.

Let them paint long strokes of brown, about 30cm from the bottom of the paper, to represent the wood for the bonfire, and then, using the fire colours, paint flames shooting upwards. They can paint the flames with sponges or large brushes. Encourage them to include some thin brush strokes for variety and realism. Do talk about fire as you work. See how many descriptive words you can introduce, through the children's own experience, and write these on separate pieces of yellow paper, cut into flame shapes, which can be pinned around the bonfire painting when it is dry.

To add figures watching the bonfire, either draw outlines of figures on the black paper or draw round some of the children to make silhouettes which can then be cut out. Several can be pinned in front of the bonfire. Bell out the figures slightly before fixing them to give a three-dimensional effect. Decorate the edge of the picture with a frill of zigzagged red crêpe paper and pin cardboard sparkling fireworks (see previous activity) along the bottom and sides too.

Thanksgiving

Thanksgiving is celebrated in the United States of America and Canada on the fourth Thursday in November. It is a time when families gather together for a special meal of traditional food such as turkey and pumpkin pie. It is a kind of harvest festival and many other blessings are remembered too.

The first people to celebrate Thanksgiving were the Pilgrim Fathers, who left England to set up home in America in 1619. Conditions were very bad and many people died. The Governor, William Bradford, was so relieved to see the harvest gathered in that he ordered a three day feast. The local Indians were also invited to share in the feast and they brought turkeys as part of their contribution. The meal was eaten outdoors on huge tables. The custom spread throughout New England and President Abraham Lincoln declared that it should be celebrated throughout the United States. In 1941, the celebration was fixed on the fourth Thursday in November. In Canada, Thanksgiving is also celebrated, but it is observed on the second Monday in October. For many people Thanksgiving is not just a day of feasting, but a time for reminding oneself of all the blessings received from God.

Handprint turkey

What you need
Large sheet of white paper, grey, white, red and black paints, shallow polystyrene trays, flat sponges as large as a child's hand, coloured foil.

What to do
For each colour of paint, take a polystyrene tray (such as meat is sold on in supermarkets) and place one of the flat sponges in it. Cover the sponge with paint and let it soak in. The children should make handprints by each pressing down one of their hands on the paint-soaked sponge, so that just enough paint covers the whole of their hand, and then pressing down their hand on a sheet of white paper. Make sure that you have enough handprints in each colour to make the turkey's tail. Leave the handprints to dry, and then let the children cut them out. Younger children will need help, but this task will give valuable scissor practice.

Next take a large circle of white paper (the size you want the turkey to be, and large enough to take at least one handprint from each child in the class) and start at the outer edge of the circle, sticking on a row of black handprints all the way round, then a row of white

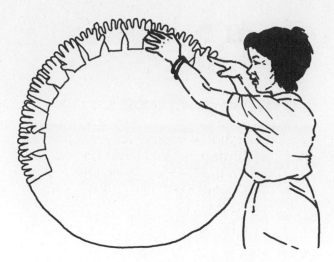

handprints inside that, and then a row of grey handprints. Repeat this pattern as you work towards the centre of the circle and make sure the coloured rows overlap a little so none of the white paper shows through.

To finish off, draw a turkey's head and body, and let the children collage this with leaf shapes cut out from paper or coloured foil. These shapes are stuck on from the bottom of the turkey's body, working upwards towards the head to give the appearance of feathers. Draw in the beak and eyes and head feathers with black paint or felt-tipped pen, and stick the finished turkey's body over the circle of printed hand shapes, so that they represent the tail feathers spread out behind.

Guru Nanak's Birthday

This Sikh festival celebrates the birthday of Guru Nanak who founded the Sikh faith. His birthday was actually in April, but is celebrated in November and for the occasion the Golden Temple of Amritsar is illuminated with hundreds of candles and lamps because Guru Nanak illuminated people's lives. The festival starts two days before the full moon in November with a continuous reading of the holy book (the Guru Granth Sahib), followed by stories of Guru Nanak's life and work.

Sikhs believe that there is one God, who is maker of all things, without fear or emnity. He is made known to men through the Guru and Sikhs regard all men as their brothers. Their temple is called a *gurdwara* and after readings from the Guru Granth Sahib, the Sikh worshippers offer hospitality to everyone, whatever their faith, in the temple kitchen, the *langar*. Their food is vegetarian.

Chapattis

What you need
Bowl, heavy frying pan, fish slice, rolling pin.
Ingredients
250g (8oz) wholemeal flour
1tsp salt
200ml (½pint) water
cooking oil

What to do
Chapattis are a traditional bread, eaten by Sikhs and other Indian peoples and are generally made freshly before being eaten.

Mix the flour and the salt in a bowl and make a small well in the centre of the mix. Gradually pour all the water into this, mixing until you have a soft dough. Knead this on a floured board for about 5 minutes then cover and leave to prove for half an hour. Divide the mixture into small portions, one for each of the children and then get them each to knead their mixture and divide it again into pieces each about the size of a very small egg. Tell the children to roll out each small piece of dough into a circle about 10cm across.

The chapattis are now ready to cook and an adult should do this. The oil should be heated on a low heat and the chapattis cooked until they blister, however they should be prevented from rising too much by being pressed down with the fish slice.

Serve the chapattis warm and suggest that the children eat them folded like a piece of bread.

Cucumber raita

What you need
Sharp knife, bowl.
Ingredients
300ml (½pint) natural yoghurt
½ cucumber
2tbsp freshly chopped mint
pinch each of salt and black pepper
Basmati rice (optional)

What to do
This is a mild and refreshing vegetable side-dish, eaten after more spicy foods.

Peel the cucumber and slice it lengthwise from top to bottom, then cut the slices into pieces about 3cm long. Mix the cucumber into the yoghurt with the other ingredients, cover and chill for about half an hour, then serve. Cut slices of cucumber for the children to dip into the mixture too.

You may also like to prepare some rice which can be eaten with the chapattis (see previous activity) and raita for a small vegetarian feast. Basmati rice is best for Indian dishes. Indian meals are made up of several dishes, each served in a small metal bowl called a *katori*. These are placed on a tray called a *thali*, with the rice in the middle. Meals like this are called *thalis*.

To remember the Sikh custom of hospitality, have the food prepared by one group of children to be served to the rest as a treat. You can talk about helping others as you work together.

St Andrew's Day

St Andrew was one of the disciples of Jesus, the brother of Simon Peter (St Peter) and a fisherman. St Andrew is the patron saint of Scotland and his feast is celebrated on 30 November. It is said that his remains were taken to Scotland by monks, and at the place where the bones were laid, St Andrew's Cathedral was built and the town of St Andrews developed.

The story goes that St Andrew was arrested for being a Christian, and because he felt that he was not worthy to die as Jesus had done, he asked that he should be crucified on a diagonal cross. This is now known as St Andrew's cross and is shown in the Scottish flag as a white cross for his purity, against a blue background to represent his connection with the sea as a fisherman. St Andrews day is a time for national celebration by Scots, no matter where they may be.

Scottish flag

What you need
White paper, blue paint (or blue paper, white paint).

What to do
With younger children, painting the white cross on a blue background will probably be the best way of creating the flag. With older children, you can talk about diagonal lines, and compare them with vertical and horizontal lines. Look for the triangles created when the diaogonal lines are drawn in a rectangle. Give the older children practice in drawing the lines using a ruler. Attach the finished flags to rolled-up paper 'flag poles'.

Fish and flag frieze

What you need
Newspapers, large tin foil pie plates, empty ball-point pens, scissors.

What to do
Place several layers of newspaper on the table and cut the rims off the pie plates. Let the children draw fish shapes on to the tin foil circles themselves or give younger ones cardboard templates to draw round. Then they should cut out the fish shapes. (You might decide to have the fish shapes cut out ready for younger children, since it is difficult for them to handle the cutting of the foil.) Next place the fish shape on the pile of newspapers and encourage the children to draw on eyes, fins and tail patterns, and to decorate the bodies of their tin foil fish with scales or wavy lines using the empty pens. They will have to be careful not to press too hard, otherwise the point of the pen may puncture the foil. When completed, the fish can be hung with the flags (see previous activity) to make a decorative frieze all around the room.

Scottish dancing

What you need
A selection of Scottish music recordings (for example, reels and highland fling) available from your local music library, tape recorder, a large space.

What to do
Play the Scottish music, its speed and gaiety will encourage the children to move. Let them get the feel of it and then introduce some simple moves, such as a large circle all going one way and changing direction as the music changes, a circle within a circle, skipping with a partner around the room holding hands with the arms over the shoulders (as in the 'Gay Gordons'), again changing direction as the music changes.

If you know anyone who has full Scottish national dress invite him or her into school to show the children. Talk about the different items which go to make the costume. This would make a useful comparison with the Five Ks of the Sikh *Khalsa*, see page 46.

Advent

The Christian year begins with the first Sunday in Advent which occurs on the fourth Sunday before Christmas. The word 'Advent' means 'coming', and this period of four weeks is a time of preparation in the Christian church for the coming of Christ, preparing for Christmas, looking to the return of Christ at the end of the world and remembering Mary's journey to Bethlehem. In the church services, there are readings from the Old Testament which Christians believe tell of the coming of a Saviour, and carols are sung such as, 'O come, O come, Emmanuel' since 'Emmanuel' means 'God with us'. Some churches have an Advent wreath, or Advent crown. This is usually a circle of evergreens which has five candles on it; three purple candles and one pink candle on the circle itself and a larger white candle in the middle. The three purple candles are said to represent penance and preparing for the coming of the Saviour. One candle is lit on the first, second and fourth Sundays of Advent. The pink candle is lit on the third Sunday (Gaudete Sunday) and represents joy. Finally, the white candle is lit on Christmas morning — the birthday of Christ, the 'Light of the World'.

For children, Advent is a time of great excitement and expectation too. They mark off the days of Advent with an Advent calendar, from 1 December to Christmas Eve (24 December). Most Advent calendars have little numbered windows set in a large seasonal picture. The children open window number one on 1 December, window number two on 2 December and so on to 24 December. During this time there are many Christmas carol services, again to remind people and help them to prepare for the coming of Christ.

Advent crown

What you need
Circle of florist's oasis, evergreen cuttings, five candles, shallow circular dish or tray, Plasticine.

What to do
Place the circle of oasis in the middle of the shallow dish. Make sure the dish is large enough to take the oasis and leave enough room to stand the candles around the outside. Use the Plasticine to position and hold the candles, four on the outside of the circle and one inside. The children can now decorate the oasis with cuttings of holly, laurel and possibly bits off the Christmas tree. They may need to wear gardening gloves when handling the holly. After each Sunday of Advent, on the Monday at a suitable time, choose one of the children to help you to light one of the candles on the Advent crown. You could also perhaps read part of the Christmas story, spread out over the four weeks. Remind the children of the dangers of fire and only have the candle burning while you read the story or talk about the meaning of Christmas. Remember to water the oasis to keep the evergreens fresh over the four weeks.

Advent calendar

What you need

Four egg boxes, sticky tape, old Christmas cards, adhesive, scissors, tissue paper, sweets.

What to do

Talk about calendars and look at the way in which the days are set out on a regular calendar. Talk about the days of the week and the months of the year, linking the seasons to different months. Give the children cards with the days or months written on and help them to sort these cards into the right order. Teach them the little rhyme, 'Thirty days hath September . . .'. Talk about the days of December and count up to 24, showing the numbers as you go.

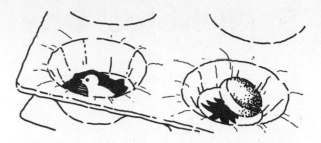

To make the Advent calendar, let the children paint the four egg boxes the colour of their choice and stick them together with tape. Meanwhile, some of the children can be cutting out small pictures from the old Christmas cards to stick in the bottom of the sections of the egg box. When the paint is dry and a small picture has been stuck in each section of the egg box, lay the boxes flat on the table and put a sweet in each egg box section. Next you will need 24 circles of tissue paper, cut to fit exactly over the rim of an egg box section and each with a number from 1 to 24. Stick a circle of tissue securely over each egg box section, sealing in the sweets. You can either position the numbers in sequence, or arrange them in a haphazard way so that the children will need to look for the correct number on the appropriate day. This will give them practice in looking at and recognising numbers.

On each day of December, choose one child to find the right number, pierce the tissue paper, and claim the sweet inside.

Alternatively, an Advent calendar can be made by decorating a small PE hoop with green crêpe paper and paper holly leaves, and then hanging round the hoop 24 small bags of sweets, wrapped in Christmas wrapping paper, each with a number on. With this calendar, the child has to look for the right number to claim the bag of sweets as a reward. As time passes the number of bags of sweets inevitably gets less, again showing that Christmas is drawing nearer.

St Nicholas' Day

The original Father Christmas or Santa Claus was St Nicholas, who was the Bishop of Myra in Asia Minor in the fourth century and was canonised for his 'good' works and miracles.

In Holland, he arrives in Amsterdam on his feast day, 6 December, to be welcomed by the Dutch royalty. With his servant, Black Peter, he parades through the streets of the city. Children hope that St Nicholas will leave a present in their shoes, but Black Peter leaves a bag of soot in the shoes of those children who have not been good. Dutch settlers took the custom of *Sinter Klaas* with them to America, where he became known as Santa Claus and his visits came to be made on Christmas Eve.

St Nicholas biscuits

What you need
Greased baking sheet, rolling pin, round-ended knife, pastry brush, pastry board.
Ingredients
400g (12oz) double crust pastry
200g (6oz) marzipan
a little flour
sugar
milk

What to do
On St Nicholas' Day, Dutch children are given St Nicholas letter biscuits.

Set the oven to 425°F/220°C or Gas Mark 7. Sprinkle the board with flour to stop the pastry sticking, then roll the pastry out thinly and cut into strips about 10cm x 2cm. Roll the marzipan into thin 'worms' and sprinkle them with a little sugar. Wrap a strip of pastry around each marzipan roll, dab a little milk along the edges of the pastry and gently press them together. Now let the children bend each roll into the shape of a letter, taking care not to break it. Some letters can be made from one piece of pastry by bending and shaping. Others will need to be made up from strips of different lengths, sticking the pieces of pastry together using the milk. Carefully place the finished letters on a greased baking sheet, leaving a little space between them. Place the tray in the centre of the oven for 10–15 minutes. When the biscuits are golden brown, take them out and remove them carefully from the tray.

Hanukah

Hanukah is a Jewish festival of lights held in December. It commemorates a time, 2000 years ago, when the Jews overcame the Emperor of Syria who forbade them to observe their holy days and desecrated the temple. The Jews set about cleaning the temple and searched for pure oil to relight the Temple light, but there was only enough for one night. However, the lamp stayed lit for eight nights, so to remember this miracle Hanukah is an eight day festival. Homes and synagogues are cleaned and an eight-branched *Menorah* (candlestick) forms a central part of the ceremonies and is a symbol of the festival. A ninth candle in the centre of the candlestick, called a 'servant candle' (*shammash*), is used to light the others. On the first night of Hanukah, the first candle is lit and prayers are offered. This is repeated on each night. The *menorah* is placed in the window of the house for all to see, a symbol of light, truth and goodness.

This is a happy, family festival with presents and games and good things to eat.

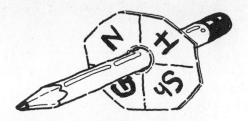

The dreidel game

What you need
White card, felt-tipped pens, old pencil, counters.

What to do
The dreidel game is a traditional Jewish game, played at this time of year. It is usually played with a four-sided spinning top with the Hebrew letters N, G, H and Sh, one on each side. These represent the motto, 'Nes Gadol Hayah Sham', which means 'A great miracle happened here.' The game is played with counters and the children start with ten each. Each child puts a counter into the 'pool' and the first player spins the top. If it lands on 'N', the child does not win anything; if it lands on 'H', half the pool is won; if it lands on 'G', the child wins the pool, and if it lands on 'Sh' the child must put a counter into the pool. The overall winner is the person with the most counters. This is an enjoyable game, with much opportunity for counting and comparison of numbers.

To make a spinner, cut out an octagon of cardboard 8cm across. Mark the centre and divide it into quarters, so that there are two facets in each quarter. You can draw this shape for the children and ask them to cut it out. An adult can make a hole in the centre of the spinner with a pair of scissors and then push a short, blunted pencil through the hole to act as the pivot, leaving an equal amount of pencil on each side. To spin the top, hold the top of the pencil and twist it round quickly in an upright position.

Potato latkes

What you need
Grater, bowl, frying pan.
Ingredients
4 large potatoes
1 egg
pinch salt and pepper
vegetable oil to fry
1 small onion (optional)

What to do
This is a traditional Jewish dish eaten at this time of year. The oil used to fry the latkes reminds the people of the little oil left in the temple jar.

Grate the potatoes quite coarsely and put them in a bowl of cold water straight away, to prevent them going brown and soggy. Next beat the egg and add the seasoning. Having drained the potato well, add the seasoned egg to the potato. Heat the oil in a frying pan and fry a tablespoon of the potato mixture at a time for about 5 minutes.

Drain the latkes well and serve them straight away.

Recipes vary and usually have a little grated onion or cheese added, but this may be too strong a taste for the youngest children.

St Lucia's Day

In some European countries the Christmas celebrations begin on St Lucia's Day, 13 December. St Lucia came from Sicily, where she was put to death by the Romans for her Christian beliefs. In Italy, her feast day is still celebrated with a fire festival, and there are processions by torch and candlelight. 'Fire' festivals are common worldwide in winter and 'Lucia' means 'light'.

In Sweden, she is known as the patron saint of light. Each town has its own Lucia Queen, who walks from house to house, and visits hospitals, wearing a long white dress with a red sash round her waist. On her head, she has a crown of bilberry and other evergreen twigs and seven lighted candles. The evergreens represent life continuing through winter. She is accompanied by her white clad attendants; girls with tinsel in their hair, and boys, representing her brothers (Star boys), wearing tall cone-shaped hats covered with gold and silver stars.

Each family will also have its own celebration. It is usually the youngest girl in the family who wakes her parents at first light with a breakfast of coffee, Lucia buns and ginger snaps (*pepparkakor*).

Make a St Lucia crown

What you need
Thin gold card, thin white card, scraps of red metallic card or foil, adhesive, scissors, staple gun, sprigs of evergreen (optional).

What to do
Cut a strip of gold card 6cm deep and long enough to go around the Lucia Queen's head with a 3cm overlap. Cut out seven rectangles of white card 8cm x 3cm and seven red, metallic flame shapes with a flat tab at one end. Stick the flames to the white rectangles, and attach the 'candles' to the inside of the headband, spacing them equally apart. Close the headband to fit the child's head and staple it to secure it, then staple on little sprigs of evergreen around the gold band.

St Lucia parade

What you need
Props and costumes for Lucia Queen, attendants and Star boys.

What to do
Pick a girl to be the Lucia Queen by drawing her name from a hat, the other children can be the attendants and Star boys. The children will need to be dressed in white. Make a crown for the Lucia Queen, and a tinsel headband for each one of the Queen's attendants. Make cone-shaped hats for the Star boys, decorated with gold and silver stars. You may wish to make some of the St Lucia Day recipes and process around school, giving out the cakes and biscuits as you go.

As you process, sing the song, 'Now light one thousand Christmas lights', a traditional Swedish song arranged by H. and R. Shekerjian, in *Merrily to Bethlehem* (1978, A&C Black) edited by D. Gadsby and I. Golby.

A recipe for St Lucia buns can be found in *Bright Ideas: Festivals* by Jill Bennett and Archie Millar (1988, Scholastic) and for Pepparkakor biscuits in *Bright Ideas for Early Years: Christmas Art and Craft* by Rhona Whiteford and Jim Fitzsimmons (1992, Scholastic).

Christmas

The most widely celebrated Christian festival is Christmas. It is celebrated on 25 December in both secular and religious ways. The name comes from the old English, 'Cristes Maesse', or 'Christ's Mass' and it celebrates the birth of Jesus Christ. During the weeks before, many schools and children's groups practise Nativity plays, which tell the story of the events surrounding the birth of Christ, and which they perform for parents and relatives as part of the Christmas preparations and celebrations. Nativity plays have developed from medieval mummers' and miracle plays. In most churches a crib is set up. This is a model of the stable where Christ was born, and it contains the figures of Mary, the mother of Jesus, and Joseph, her husband, with an ox and an ass. On Christmas Eve, there is the ceremony in some churches of the 'Blessing of the crib', when the figure of the infant Jesus is placed in the manger, and the figures of the shepherds and sometimes the Three Wise Men or Kings are placed in as well. After this, the Midnight Mass is celebrated with readings from the Gospel telling the story of the birth of Christ, and the singing of 'carols', special songs which also tell of the birth of Jesus.

Many of the customs associated with Christmas are a result from it taking place at the time of the winter solstice. This was traditionally a time for feasting and celebration linked to the Roman festival of 'Saturnalia'. Other customs came from Europe, such as the Yule log, decorating the house with evergreens and the Christmas tree. The first Christmas tree was brought to England by Prince Albert for Queen Victoria. The tradition of sending cards is thought to have started in England, and these days a great industry has grown to supply people with decorations, trees, festive lights and cards to decorate their homes and shops.

Most young children believe that Father Christmas or Santa Claus brings presents for them on Christmas morning, and Christmas Day is a time when families try to be together. They eat a special Christmas meal which varies worldwide, but in Britain is usually turkey, with vegetables and a sage and onion stuffing, followed by a rich, fruit Christmas pudding or Christmas cake. Other treats at this time include mince pies and chocolate log (originally a French Christmas tradition). Most people believe that Christmas is also a time for thinking about others less fortunate than themselves and many people contribute to charity at this time.

Christmas log

What you need
Mixing bowl, wooden spoon, sieve, double-boiler, cake board, round-ended knife, fork, holly and robin cake decorations (optional).
Ingredients
1 chocolate Swiss roll
12g (4oz) butter or margarine
180g (6oz) icing sugar
30g (1–1½oz) melted cooking chocolate
2 drops of vanilla essence

What to do
Many foods are associated with Christmas and one of the favourites is the chocolate log. This is a reminder of the old custom of dragging home the Yule log, which was meant to be large enough to be lit on Christmas Eve and last the entire 12 days of Christmas.

Cream the butter until soft and beat in the sieved icing sugar a little at a time until it is all incorporated, then add the vanilla essence. Melt the chocolate in a double-boiler and fold the melted chocolate into the butter and icing sugar, mixing it well with the wooden spoon. Leave the mixture to cool.

Place the Swiss roll on a cake board, and cover the surface of the roll with the cooled chocolate butter icing. Create the bark effect by dragging the prongs of a fork over the butter icing along the length of the roll. Sprinkle the cake with a little icing sugar to give the appearance of snow, and decorate it with a sprig of holly and a Christmas robin cake decoration.

Christmas Nativity

What you need
Simple props (such as decorated boxes for the gifts of the Three Wise Men, a small box for the manger, a baby doll from the role-play centre, toy lambs that the children may be able to bring in and so on), basic Nativity costumes (such as head-dresses for Mary, Joseph, the innkeepers and the shepherds, cloaks for the Kings, circlets of tinsel for the angels).

What to do
Tell or read a simplified, outline version of the Nativity story. As you read about Mary and Joseph, let the children perform the actions; such as the travelling to Bethlehem, the innkeepers turning them away, the shepherds being first to be told by the angels about Jesus' birth and then going to see him, and the Three Wise Men or Kings following a star to take their gifts to Jesus. As the children get used to the actions, you can leave them to act out the story as part of their play situations. Alternatively, you can tape the story and let them play it back and act it out as they listen.

There are many versions of the Christmas story available which are suitable for older children to perform, either for an assembly or for parents as a school play.

Book list

A Hindu Family in Britain S. Ray (1986, RMEP)

A Jewish Family in Britain V. Barnett (1983, RMEP)

A Musical Calendar of Festivals B. Cass-Beggs (Comp.) (1983, Ward Lock Educational)

A Muslim Family in Britain S. W. Harrison and D. Shepherd (1979, RMEP)

A Sikh Family in Britain W. Owen Cole (1985, RMEP)

Bright Ideas: Easter activities J. Fitzsimmons (1988, Scholastic)

Bright Ideas: Festivals J. Bennett and A. Millar (1988, Scholastic)

Festival. Diwali and Ramadan and Eid-ul-Fitr O. Bennett (1986, Commonwealth Institute/Macmillan Education)

Festivals J. Gilbert (1986, Oxford Publications)

Festivals and Celebrations K. Elliot (1984, Young Library)

Festivals and Celebrations R. W. Purton (1981, Blackwell)

Festivals and Saints Days V. J. Green (1978, Blandford Press)

Festivals in World Religions A. Brown (Ed.) (1986, Longman)

Follow the Year M. Powers (1985, Hodder and Stoughton)

Hinduism V. P. Kanitkar (1985, Wayland)

Living Festivals: Hindu festivals J. Mayled (1988, RMEP)

Religions of the World: The Buddhist world A. Bancroft (1992, Simon and Schuster Young Books)

Religions of the World: The Muslim world R. Tames (1992, Simon and Schuster Young Books)

Seasons of Splendour M. Jaffrey (1992, Puffin)

Useful Addresses

The Council of Christians and Jews, 1 Dennington Park Road, London NW6 1AX.

South London Multi-Faith Religious Education Centre, Kilmorie Road, London SE23 2SP.

The Centre for the Study of Religion and Education in the Inner City, Sacred Trinity Centre, Chapel Street, Salford, Great Manchester M3 7AJ.

Minority Group Support Service, Southfields, South Street, Coventry CV1 5EJ.

Articles of Faith, The Bury Business Centre, Kay Street, Bury BL9 6BU — for authentic religious artefacts.

Shap Working Party, c/o The National Society's Religious Education Centre, 23 Kensington Square, London W8 5HN — for the *Shap Calendar of Religious Festivals*.

The Hindu Centre, 39 Grafton Terrace, London NW5 4JA.

The Commonwealth Institute, Kensington High Street, London W8 6NQ.